Shabnam Minwalla has spent most of her life with words—editing her school magazine, working as a journalist with the *Times of India* and writing non-fiction. Her first book, *The Six Spellmakers of Dorabji Street*, was critically acclaimed and won the Rivokids Parents' and Kids' Choice Award. Apart from the Nimmi series, her books for younger readers include *The Shy Supergirl*, *Lucky Girl* and *When Jiya Met Urmila* (Winner, Neev Book Award). Her books for young adults include *What Maya Saw* (nominated for the Crossword Book Award, the Neev Book Award and the Peekabook Award), *Saira Zariwala Is Afraid* (Winner, AttaGalatta Bangalore Lit Fest Award), *Murder at Daisy Apartments* and *Zen* (both winners, Auther Award for Children's Book of the Year).

Shabnam has also written short stories in a number of anthologies, a stack of picture books and a non-fiction book, *Colaba*.

Also by Shabnam Minwalla in
Talking Cub/Speaking Tiger YA:

Nimmi's Spectabulous Schooldays
Nimmi's Dreadtastic Detective Days
Nimmi's Bizuper Birthday
Nimmi's Crawful Camping Days

Murder at Daisy Apartments

THE CHICKEN POX CLUB INVESTIGATES

The BODY in the SWIMMING POOL

SHABNAM MINWALLA

talking CUB
An Imprint of Speaking Tiger Books

TALKING CUB
Published by Speaking Tiger Books LLP
125A, Ground Floor, Shahpur Jat,
Near Asiad Village, New Delhi - 110 049

Published in Talking Cub by Speaking Tiger Books in paperback in 2024

ISBN: 978-93-5447-842-0
eISBN: 978-93-5447-885-7

10 9 8 7 6 5 4 3 2 1

Typeset in Lora by Jojy Philip
Printed at Chaman Enterprises, New Delhi

This is a work of fiction. Names, characters, places and incidents either are the product of the author's imagination or are used fictitiously, and any resemblance to actual persons, living or dead, events or locales is entirely coincidental.

Contents

An account of the first case solved by the Chicken Pox Club. Compiled in May 2023 from notes, interviews, voice recordings, diary entries and observations.

Sources used in this account include:

Poems of Strength and Courage edited by Marylou Winslow

The Detective's Bible by Alfred Roonig and Dan Hodder

The View from a High Window by Sandra Saldanha

I have tried to be as honest and accurate as possible. If, in the process, I have offended anyone, I would like to say that it was not my intention.

Paromita Mehta

Founder member

The Chicken Pox Club

30 May 2023

A Most Unpleasant Evening

Sunday, May 7

Sunday evenings are grim. The light is thin and grey, the air is heavy, and the mood is as soggy as wet socks.

The evening of May 7 was all of this and more.

The sky that pressed against my bedroom window was a fluorescent purple that made me think of plastic flowers and particulate pollution. The honks and shouts from the people on the road—after too many frappuccinos in the tummy and too many hours in the mall—sounded loud and aggressive even on the 49th floor.

The scatter of boils made my arms sore and itchy. And the deliberate vagueness with which my father announced that he was heading out for a drink with 'a friend' made my mood sorer and itchier. 'Which friend?' I brooded, convinced that he was going out with the one person that I didn't want him to go out with. 'What's he hiding?'

All this, though, was just the backdrop to the real crisis. The disaster du jour.

The missing scrap of paper. Which after two hours of hunting had continued to remain missing. And had no business going missing in the first place.

I had placed the piece of paper in the front right corner of my dressing table drawer last evening. (Four people had seen me do it.)

I had used a brown ceramic cow with a smug expression as a paperweight. (The same four people had seen me place the cow, and one of the four had passed sniggery remarks about my 'OCD' tendencies.)

Over the next twenty-four hours, I had opened the dressing table drawer just twice. Once to pull out a scrunchy. Once to put away a butterfly clip. So I was unprepared for the nasty shock awaiting me at 4 p.m. on Sunday evening.

I had just finished reading A *Good Girl's Guide to Murder* on my Kindle. (We're not going anywhere this summer. Not even Alibag or Matheran. Which is why my father, in a fit of guilt and foolhardiness, told me that I could buy up to 125 books over the holidays. I've made the most of this offer. I've already spent as much as a round trip to Delhi and by the time summer is done, I plan to spend as much as a round trip to Singapore.)

A *Good Girl's Guide to Murder* had put me in a clue-cracking, case-solving mood—which is why I decided to tackle the clue that was so obligingly sitting in my dressing table drawer.

I laid out my pencil box and my old HDFC Bank diary on my desk. Then I walked to the dressing table, pulled open the drawer and blinked. Then I rummaged around the drawer and blinked some more. But no amount of rummaging and blinking changed things.

The paper had vanished. As had the left ear of the ceramic cow.

It was a puzzle—and no matter how much I pondered, I could only come up with two rather unsatisfactory solutions.

Solution One: The paper had escaped without help. It had biffed the ceramic cow on the left ear, hopped out of the drawer, and scurried away into a dusty corner. (9/10 on the Improbability Index.)

Solution Two: The paper had escaped with help. Someone had crept into my bedroom, opened my dressing table drawer, manhandled the ceramic cow, ignored my diamond earrings and ruby bracelet, and tiptoed away with the muddy, crumply scrap of paper. (10/10 on the Improbability Index.)

No matter how the paper had vanished, however, I had to find it before the next meeting of the Chicken Pox Club. Which meant that I had to pull myself together and get down to work.

Whenever I encounter a problem in Physics or English Literature or Algebra, I begin with the relevant textbook—*Selina Concise Physics*, *Wonder of Words* or whatever. When it comes to investigating, I guess the closest thing I have to a textbook is *The Detective's Bible* by Alfred Roonig and Dan Hodder. So that is where I decided to start.

Pulling out my Xeroxed and spiral-bound copy of *The Detective's Bible*, I leafed through the pages before alighting on a chapter called, 'The Ten Rules of Sensible Sleuthing'.

The First Rule of Sensible Sleuthing is to seek clues in obvious places. So that is what I did. I hunted high and low. I examined my bookshelves and the spidery space beneath my bed. I emptied two drawers, checked behind curtains and peered under rugs. An hour later, all I had for my trouble was a dust-induced sniffle and a very bad feeling.

The Second Rule of Sensible Sleuthing is to interrogate the obvious suspects. In this case, there were only two obvious suspects. I hurried out of my bedroom and accosted both.

Meena didi was Obvious Suspect No. 1.

She sniffed and said that she never touched my things. That she had stopped touching them since the day I had called her meddlesome and colour blind. Then she sniffed some more to show that she was still offended, even though my outburst had taken place five whole months ago.

(Okay, fine! It's true that I'd overreacted when Meena didi put my charcoal grey T-shirt in the black T-shirt pile. But it's also true that Meena didi overreacted to my overreaction. She spent the next fortnight slamming doors, crashing pans, and doling out cold tea and warm nimbu pani. I didn't want a repeat of the cold-tea treatment, so I didn't question her further, even though Alfred Roonig and Dan Hodder clearly expected me to do so.)

My father was Obvious Suspect No. 2.

He pointed out that he never dared to touch my stuff. Then he suggested that I may have forgotten where I put the paper. This was so ridiculous that I could only stare at him, widen my eyes, and ask, 'Really?'

To which he could only look apologetic and mumble, 'Probably not.'

Anybody who has met me for ten minutes knows that I am not a misplacer of objects, a forgetter of names, a muddler of facts. Anybody who has spent a little more time with me understands why my school nickname is Meht-iculous.

I dislike nicknames. But if I must have one then Meht-iculous is better than Mehtallica or Par-abola or something. Firstly, it's accurate. Secondly, it's tricky to pronounce, so most people end up using my real name instead.

My real name, incidentally, is Paromita Mehta.

I am fourteen years old.

My IQ is 147, which is more than Barack Obama but considerably less than Albert Einstein and Sherlock Holmes. (I'm working on it. It's possible.)

I am left-brained. High on logic, low on imagination. (Which is fine by me.)

The adjectives that are most often used to describe me are bright, bossy and capable. (Which is also fine by me.)

I am four feet and ten inches tall and hoping for a growth spurt. My hair is straight and cut in a bob. (My Nani tells me I'm pretty and that I look like my mother, but I can't see it.)

My favourite colour is a greeny aqua. My favourite fruit is mango. My least favourite vegetable is cauliflower.

My only hobby is reading.

My favourite book of the moment is *Miss Peregrine's Home for Peculiar Children*. My favourite book of forever is *Catcher in the Rye*. (I managed to borrow it from the 'Only with Permission' shelf in the school library when our dragon librarian had dengue. Otherwise, I would've had to wait another two years to read it.)

I live on the 49th floor of Banyan Towers, which is one of four buildings in a complex called The Orchard by Kotecha. (Yes. It's the same complex that's been on the front page of all the newspapers this week. But not the same building. The murder took place in Maple Towers, though we all share the same swimming pool. Unfortunately.)

I am a student at All Saints School. Once the school year starts, I will be in Grade 9.

On that purple Sunday evening, though, school was still forty-four days away. The summer holidays had barely begun, and I was in my green-blue bedroom, swallowing Crocin, watching the sky turn into tar, and feeling agitated.

It was to calm myself that I uncapped a black gel pen, opened the HDFC Bank diary to a blank page and began to write. Everything. No matter how insignificant. No matter how irrelevant.

I wrote about the birth of the Chicken Pox Club and our first assignment. About the grimy sheet of paper that Nihal Advani had produced from his backpack. About all the people who had floated through my apartment in the last twenty-four hours. About the conversations we had had and the observations we had made.

And, of course, I wrote about Sandra Saldanha.

The Eighth Rule of Sensible Sleuthing states that the moment you start a new case, you must make detailed notes. And it was becoming increasingly apparent that the Chicken Pox Club had just embarked on its first case—even if I had managed to lose its first clue.

How It All Began

The events leading up to **Thursday, May 4**

The Orchard by Kotecha comprises four sixty-four-storeyed, silverish, bean-shaped buildings. The buildings are arranged like the blades of a ceiling fan around a vast, round swimming pool.

Although the complex is named The Orchard, it has more buildings than trees. To make up for this, Mr Kotecha has named the buildings after trees. Banyan, Gulmohar, Cedar and Maple. (Neither a maple nor a cedar could possibly survive in the heat and dust of Parel, but Mr Kotecha is not one to bother with details like natural habitats.)

Five hundred and seven families live in The Orchard. Most of them live here, not because the buildings are impersonating trees, but because of the swimming pool and the tennis courts and the library and the grocery store and the temple and the Starbucks and the expensive French restaurant and the free shuttle to the mall and the in-house doctor.

'Worth it for the facilities,' the adults gloat, whenever they queue up for the lift with their Vanilla Lattes. 'We don't need to leave the complex only. All amenities are right here.'

Whenever I overhear such comments, I do a mental eyeroll.

Just think about it. The doctor in question is Dr Prabhu, a pasty-faced individual who mewls at the sight of blood. (Before him, it was the eighty-four-year-old Dr Saxena, who was forced to retire three months ago after he started prescribing jumbled-up mantras and cow ghee instead of medicine.)

The library in question has never heard of A *Wrinkle in Time*. 'Is it a part of the Geronimo Stilton series?' the librarian asked me last week before feebly pawing through the shelves of Dan Brown, self-help books and crumbling volumes bequeathed by the families of Mr Menon and Dr Kavaksh (both of whom died last year after being treated by the dubious, incorrect-mantra-prescribing Dr Saxena).

The swimming pool in question has made it to all the newspapers under headlines like 'Pool of Horror' and 'Dive of Death'.

And the keep-children-busy-in-summer amenity is the Kotecha's Summer Selebrations, which offers expensive workshops with misleading names like 'Swim your way to the Olympics' and 'Paint like Picasso'.

Every summer, parents rush to enroll their children in the workshops, while saying in smugger-than-usual voices:

'Keeps them occupied. Otherwise, they get so bored.'

'Otherwise they spend the whole day on their devices. So bad for the eyes.'

'It was for these facilities only that we moved to The Orchard.'

During the four years that I have lived in Banyan Towers, I have staunchly refused to be a part of the Kotecha Summer Selebrations. I am not interested in fitness, Bollywood dance, swimming or art. I abhor deliberate misspellings. And I can't imagine anything more humiliating than the Summer Selebration Finale for which Mr Kotecha descends from his lofty heights—an obese penthouse protruding from the terrace of Maple Towers—and distributes certificates with one hand while holding phone to ear with the other.

I had planned to spurn the Selebrations this year too, but changed my mind when I spotted a poster in the library. The poster sported a bloody knife, a gun, and a bottle bearing the label 'Deadly Cyanide'. This is what it said:

Summer Selebration Surprise! 'The Clue Crew'
Presenting, for the first time, a workshop for young detectives.

In this you will learn how to:

- Examine the scene of the murder
- Listen to what the corpse is telling you
- Get introduced to new technologies
- Analyze body-language and handwriting

Unique opportunity: Meet Prakash Talwar, Mumbai's foremost detective and ask him about his cases and his strategies.

Free upon registration: one magnifying glass, one fingerprint kit and one copy of *The Detective's Bible*.

Number of sessions: 12

Course facilitator: Rehana Iqbal, MS in Forensic Science from Nottingham Trent University, UK.

Capacity: 15

Hurry to book your slot and avoid disappointment!!!!

Whenever people ask me what I plan to become when I grow up, I say that I want to be a physicist and research dark matter. But sometimes—in my more frivolous moments—I daydream about being a detective.

I must have been in a frivolous mood that day because I did what the poster suggested. I hurried to book my slot and avoid disappointment.

The Clue Crew workshop started on the first Saturday of the summer holidays. It was held every morning from 10 a.m. to 1 p.m. We missed one class on Tuesday because the murder had just taken place and the parents on the Summer Selebration chat got hysterical and The Orchard was crawling with policemen. Otherwise, though, we were diligent and regular.

The sessions were conducted by Miss Rehana, but we had guest speakers like Mr Darabsha from Pune, who told us about handwriting analysis, and a psychologist from Chembur, who told us about body language. (Did you know that a pointy handwriting is a sign of someone who is ambitious? Or that people tend to scratch, fidget or rock when they are lying? Or that a person who is gesticulating with two hands is more likely to be lying than a person who is gesticulating with one hand?)

Prakash Talwar's talk was scheduled for next week. I googled him and found that he was part of an agency called 'Talwar Kumar Investigations' and that he was a big deal. He'd cracked an art fraud racket a couple of years ago; he'd figured out the person behind a series of assaults in a famous Goa hotel; and he'd nabbed a jewel thief during the Zaveri-Mangaldas wedding. It made sense that so many celebrity weddings and luxury buildings in Mumbai—including The Orchard by Kotecha—used him as a security consultant.

I'm not prone to fan-girling, but I was excited about meeting Prakash Talwar. (I was sort of hoping that he would find me so intelligent and perceptive that he would offer me an internship on the spot.)

I don't like people easily, but I liked Miss Rehana.

I don't make friends quickly, but I got along with Tarini from Gulmohar Towers.

Everything was happening as it should.

And then suddenly everything was happening as it shouldn't, all because of eleven reddish bumps.

The eleven bumps made their appearance on Thursday night.

The minute I noticed them, I knew. It didn't take Sherlock-Holmes-level skills to figure out what the bumps meant. It didn't even take Miss-Rehana-the-forensic-expert-without-a-job-level skills to figure out what they meant.

Just hours before the eleven bumps made their appearance on my stomach and my shoulders, my father's phone had lit up with four messages. All the messages were on the Summer Selebration Workshops chat. All the messages were bearers of bad news.

Shaila Vora: Aggu has had boils for some days. Had him checked and he has been diagnosed with chicken pox. Thought it best to inform

Mita Menon: Sunidhi also woke up with boils today. I imagine chicken pox as well. Such a pain because things crazy at work so am hardly at home. Such bad luck she can't attend the workshop. What a way to start their summer holidays. Hope others not sick as well. Poor dears.

Diana Engineer: Oh. Darius woke up with boils this morning. Guess he too has chicken pox?

Melly Advani: Nihal too.

I didn't know Sunidhi Menon, and I didn't know which Summer Selebration workshop she was in. So that was fine.

I did know Agastya Vora, but I didn't know which workshop he was in. (Probably swimming or fitness, given that he was one of those boys with three brain cells and 30,000 muscles.) So that was fine too.

I did know Darius Engineer and Nihal Advani and I did know which workshop they were in. And that really wasn't fine.

Like me, Darius Engineer and Nihal Advani had signed up for 'The Clue Crew'. Like me, they had spent the last week learning about fingerprints, blood splatters and cadavers. Like me, they had spent their mornings in the close, air-conditioned confines of Conference Room D in the basement of Cedar Towers.

There was no escaping it. If Darius Engineer and Nihal Advani had chicken pox, so did I.

Varicella Zoster Does Its Thing

Friday, May 5

A miserable, headachy day. Many reasons to feel sorry for myself. More papules. (Wish now that I hadn't googled the stages of chicken pox. Papules sound much more sore and diseased than bumps or boils.)

Dr Prabhu confirmed the diagnosis on Friday morning. He peered at my papules from a nervous distance, and then acted like he was making the revelation of the millennium—a sort of medical equivalent of Copernicus announcing that the Earth revolves around the Sun. 'I would say...when I put everything together...that it is probably chicken pox...'

Surprise, surprise!

Dr Prabhu is, as I've already mentioned, the doctor for The Orchard by Kotecha and The Arboretum by Kotecha. I always wondered why any doctor would want to spend his life at the beck and call of the residents of seven rich and entitled buildings in Central Mumbai. I stopped wondering after encountering Dr Prabhu a couple of times.

Dr Prabhu is in his forties. He's one of those people who is incapable of looking you in the eye and giving you a clear answer. I find it impossible to trust a doctor who has entire conversations with my left shoulder and who, when I crossly tell him that I've had both doses of chicken pox vaccination, nods at my left shoulder and says, 'Very nice. Very nice.'

Very nice, very nice?

Would you blame me for being in a funk?

I was itchy and unwell.

I was mad about missing seven sessions of The Clue Crew. I'd been looking forward to the talk by Prakash Talwar; and I'd been waiting for the 'Solve the Crime Scene' challenge, because I'm certain I would have won it. (The prize is a Rs 1000 Amazon gift coupon, which would mean three more books.)

If that was not bad enough, I was being treated by a doctor who talked to my left shoulder and who thought it was very nice that I'd managed to get chicken pox although I was fully vaccinated.

And if even that was not bad enough, I had to sit around being itchy, feverish, and bitter in the company of two gremlinish, germ-laden boys. All thanks to my busybody father.

About twenty minutes after Dr Prabhu collected his fee and left, my father sidled into the living room and cleared his throat. He asked how I was feeling. I told him that I was feeling pretty much the same as I'd felt ten minutes ago. Then he delivered his news, after which I felt considerably worse than I'd felt ten minutes ago.

'Miss Rehana has promised to send you some puzzles and crime-solving exercises,' my father said, as he pulled on his socks and got ready to leave the house.

I brightened up at that. Miss Rehana conducts The Clue Crew class. She knows all about blood splatters, sweat deposits and tyre treads and has been giving us mind-boggling mysteries to discuss. (On Wednesday, we discussed the mystery of the twenty-one severed, sneaker-wearing feet that had washed up on the coast of the US and Canada. There are many theories, and we went through them in detail. I was most disappointed that the psycho-with-foot-obsession theory was probably the wrong one.)

'That's very sweet of—' I started to say when my father spoke again.

'Then Miss Rehana had an even better idea,' he said. 'She thought that it would be good for some of you to form a Detective Club.'

'It would,' I said, shedding my newfound brightness and feeling mopey all over again. 'But it's impossible. Most people are planning to travel. They won't want to risk getting chicken pox and—'

'Don't worry about all that,' my father said airily. 'I've solved that problem.'

'How?' I snorted, skepticism replacing self-pity. My father usually leaves his problem-solving abilities at the office, along with his business cards, his jar of seeds and his posh voice.

'I've invited Darius Engineer and Nihal Advani to come over for the next week,' my father explained. 'They also have chicken pox, and they also enjoy this detective business. It's the best solution for everyone.'

Best solution for everyone? Like seriously?

I yelled and stamped and declared that over my chicken-poxy dead body would I be in a club with a notorious vandal (Darius Engineer) and a boy who had less personality than a block of tofu (Nihal Advani).

I said that I'd rather form a Detective Club with a slimy hagfish and a sea cucumber. (Though maybe not. If a hagfish doesn't like you, it releases enough slime into the water to clog your eyes, mouth, and nose—which really isn't a nice way to die. Sea cucumbers are gross rather than devious. They breathe through their anuses. Despite their many faults, Darius Engineer and Nihal Advani aren't slime-releasing anus breathers.)

My father usually does what I tell him to do, but not this time. He mumbled something about it being important for me to spend time with other children. Then he mumbled something about the boys being here in ten minutes and staying for lunch. After which he stopped mumbling so that he could yank on his shoes. Then, without bothering with shoelaces or fond farewells, he fled to his office.

Ten minutes later, there were two chicken-poxy boys sitting in my bedroom, scratching their papules, fiddling with my telescope and generally being a nuisance.

I refused to play gracious hostess. I was unfriendly and determined to prove that I was cleverer and quicker at solving Miss Rehana's puzzles. That I was a superior being in every way.

This had an unfortunate effect on my two guests. Darius Engineer became louder and more obnoxious than usual. He cracked revolting jokes and sang revolting songs. Nihal Advani became more silent and invisible than usual. There were long stretches of the morning during which Darius sang tunelessly, Nihal sat like the winner of a statue impersonating contest and I thought nasty thoughts.

A bad time was had by all.

It was a couple of hours after Darius Engineer and Nihal Advani left that Miss Rehana sent us our first challenge. 'Task 1,' she posted on the Detective Club chat.

Miss Rehana: Each of you needs to find a mystery. It could be something you read in the newspaper. Or a blood-stained knife that you find in your flowerpot. Or something off at school.

Miss Rehana: It must be something you can actually investigate. So no schoolgirls missing in Finland or emeralds stolen 500 years ago in Turkey.

Miss Rehana: Bring your mysteries in on Saturday morning and discuss them. If you were to investigate one mystery, which would you choose? I'll come in around lunchtime to see what you have.

At first, I was disappointed because the challenge seemed so simple. But I soon found that sometimes it's more difficult to spot a mystery than to solve it.

A Most Eventful Morning

Saturday, May 6

More papules. A few pustules. And one more person in my bedroom—a chicken poxy girl.

Sunidhi Menon landed up with a box of brownies, about 300 reddish bumps, a ponytail and an unexpectedly fat laugh that came from somewhere deep inside her. Her mother had called my father and asked if Sunidhi could be part of 'the little chicken pox club'. And my father had extended a warm welcome without bothering to check with me. (This was getting to be a bad habit.)

Everything about Sunidhi bounced—her ponytail, her voice, her body, her mood. She didn't seem to mind spending the morning with one intimidating girl, one vandal and one invisible boy. She giggled and talked and made herself most at home.

'Too funny. I signed up for the dance workshop, but I've landed up in a Detective Club. I think it will be much nicer. I thought we would have the Dance

Monkeys people as usual. But this year dance is being taught by two very mean instructors called Miss Heena and Sir Renato. Have you noticed that dance teachers and swimming teachers are the worst? Miss Heena has been body-shaming everyone. She told me that my legs are too short. Do you think my legs are too short? And if they are too short then too short for what?'

It was a good thing that Sunidhi didn't expect an answer because we were incapable of giving her one. We sat dumbstruck while she rattled on. 'Miss Heena is obsessed with the Butterfly Leap. She acts like if you can't do the Butterfly Leap you can't dance. I'm determined to get it just to show her. And that Renato is useless. What is the point of a dance teacher who can't dance?'

All this before she had even reached the middle of the room.

Sunidhi stopped speaking for a moment while she put the box of brownies on my desk and sat down cross-legged on the blue rug. The pause gave Darius Engineer a chance to point out that at least she wasn't in the swimming class.

This set Sunidhi off again.

She laughed, though it really wasn't a laughing matter. Then she talked some more. 'Yes, seriously. I don't think I could bear to step into that pool for a month or two. Could you? They only shut it for two days. Isn't two days too little? I mean, this is worse than the time Baby Jaden pottied in the pool and all the parents signed that letter. They should, at least, have stopped the swimming class. You know Meher Tampal from Gulmohar Towers?'

I said I didn't. Darius said he did. Nihal didn't say anything.

'Meher had a panic attack when the teacher told her to enter the pool. She started shaking so much that she had to be carried back home. I don't blame her one bit—is your room always so neat, or is it in our honour? I like the blue and green theme. I'm going to take pictures to show my mom. My room is very pink and princess, but I think I'm over pink and princess. Aren't you?'

I said that I'd never been into pink or princess, which made Sunidhi laugh and bounce all over again. 'Oh Paromita,' she cried. 'You are too, too funny.'

I found Sunidhi baffling but both Darius Engineer and Nihal Advani looked happier now that she and her box of brownies had made their way into our Detective Club.

The box of brownies, incidentally, played a central role in our history. Mrs Menon had taped a card on the parcel and addressed it to: The Chicken Pox Club.

The name stuck.

I disapproved. But there was a lot that I disapproved of even more, starting with Darius Engineer.

Darius Engineer is a thirteen-year-old boy with Bambi eyes, long eyelashes, and an air of innocence.

He lives on the 55th floor of Banyan Towers. As is so often the case, the long lashes and innocence are misleading. When we first moved into Banyan Towers four years ago, we were harassed by doorbells in the dead of the night and menacing notes—of the 'I kno evrything' and 'Fier for your Life' variety—slipped under our door.

Whenever I imagined the writer of those notes, I pictured a burly, moustachioed individual with an eyepatch and a prominent scar. It was a shock when the perpetrator turned out to be the angelic, lisping boy who lived six floors above us.

Darius Engineer is bigger now. He's no longer the automatic choice for the angel in a Christmas play. He no longer slips misspelt notes under doors. But he still spells/misspells trouble.

I was not thrilled when Darius popped up in The Clue Crew workshop. I was even less thrilled when he popped up in my bedroom along with a menagerie of rubber spiders, cockroaches, and a revoltingly realistic plastic poop.

I'm able to ignore the spiders and cockroaches. I'm even able to overlook the poop. But I cannot stand it when Darius Engineer drones 'Who let the dogs out' in a flat monotone. It irritates me more than all the papules, pustules and scabs put together.

Darius Engineer and I rub each other the wrong way. As I get more disapproving and tight-lipped, he gets louder and more offensive. So I guess I should be grateful that Nihal Advani evens things out.

Nihal Advani is a neat, slight boy who lives in Gulmohar Towers. We've been waiting at the same bus stop and riding the same school bus for four years. Although we've never been in the same division, we've been in the same class of All Saints School for eight years.

Even so I know nothing at all about Nihal Advani. Like *nothing*, nothing.

I don't know if he plays tennis or if he has a sibling or if he's smart. It's true that I'm not very good when it comes to people. But in this case, the problem is not me—it's Nihal Advani. Not even Sunidhi can get more than a monosyllable out of him, which is saying a lot.

Sunidhi Menon has shoulder-length hair and a smiley face. She's around my age and my height, but in every other way we are different.

The minute Sunidhi walked into the house on Saturday morning, a voice in my head groaned, 'Oh no!' I instantly knew that she was one of the giggly, popular girls who spend hours sitting in Starbucks, attending Dance Nites and Game Nites and saying things like 'You do you' in an American accent.

I've never gotten along with giggly, popular, American-accented girls and they've never gotten along with me. I see them as fakes and flakes. They see me as a geek.

Sunidhi is not a flake. Despite the brand logos and 1901 Instagram followers, she's sensible and intelligent. Still, there's every chance that she's a fake. I know how these popular types operate and I will not let myself get taken in.

We Get Down to Business

Saturday, May 6

As soon as we'd eaten our brownies, I called the meeting to order.

'Let's discuss our mysteries,' I said firmly. 'I can go first.'

I had picked a newspaper article about odd rattling sounds in a building in Wadala. Nobody seemed to know if the noises were the work of a prankster or the outcome of insect infestation or structural problems. I had thought—and I still do think—that it was fascinating.

Darius Engineer disagreed loudly and jeerily. 'And the evil perpetrator of the crime of the century,' he cackled, 'is a...pigeon.'

This was rich, given that Darius Engineer's mystery was a small, shapeless metal thing. He claimed it was a bullet that he had found in The Orchard tennis court a couple of weeks ago. (Yeah right!)

Although it was Sunidhi's first day in the Detective Club, she had a suggestion. 'I don't understand why we're looking for other mysteries when the nastiest murder in the city has taken place right next to us,' she said. 'I don't know about all of you, but I'm seriously haunted. I think about it every thirty seconds and then feel sick.'

Sunidhi was, of course, referring to the murder of Sandra Saldanha that had taken place just four days ago—a ghastly incident that had put The Orchard and its swimming pool on the front page of every newspaper in the city.

Sandra Saldanha had lived on the 56th floor of Maple Towers. She had been sixty-two years old and a former professor of English at St Paul's College. She'd lived alone and quietly.

The only reason I could connect a face to her name was that I'd spoken to her a couple of times in The Orchard library. The first time was three months ago. I'd been looking through the curated-for-morons collection of children's books in the library and feeling hopeless. 'Do you have anything new?' I'd asked the librarian, a pale and limp-wristed woman whom all the children addressed as 'Miss' and all the adults addressed as 'Madam'.

The librarian had used her limp wrist to indicate a book called *Captain Underpants and the Wrath of the Wicked Wedgie Woman.*

The Captain Underpants series is huge with seven-year-old boys who crack up when they hear words like poopypants—but as I'm neither a boy nor seven years old, I wasn't a Captain Underpants fan.

'Don't you have any better books?' I sort of snapped.

The librarian did a droopy headshake.

I was about to stomp away when I heard a chuckle behind me. I turned and saw a sweet-faced woman with a grey bob and a very amused expression. 'I know exactly how you're feeling,' she told me. 'I too get crabby when I'm unable to get hold of a good book. What is your name, dear? Which school are you in? Which building do you live in? Which books are you reading at the moment?'

The sweet-faced woman was, of course, Sandra Saldanha. We chatted for about ten minutes. She told me that she'd been a college teacher all her life and that Miss Pavri, who was my English teacher at school, had been one of her star students. 'Please give her my love,' she said. 'I remember every single student I've ever taught, and I remember her particularly well.'

We discussed books for some time and Sandra Saldanha suggested that I read *Journey to the River Sea*. 'If you enjoy it,' she promised, 'I will suggest more books.'

I said that I would buy *Journey to the River Sea* with my birthday money, but Sandra Saldanha said that wasn't necessary. 'Use your birthday money to buy carrot cake,' she'd twinkled before turning to the librarian and saying, 'Vasanthi dear, I'm fetching *Journey to the River Sea* for Paromita.'

The librarian shed her limpness for a milli-second and smiled. Actually smiled!

Sandra Saldanha had walked up to a cupboard in the corner—one that I'd assumed was stuffed with dog-eared dictionaries and suchlike from the Menon/Kavaksh collection—pulled out a book and handed it to me with a jaunty wink.

I'd loved *Journey to the River Sea* and had thanked Sandra Saldanha when I met her next. She'd beamed and had pulled out *Mrs 'Arris Goes to Paris* from the same cupboard. 'Send me a message when you're done,' she'd said, and given me her phone number.

I'd saved the number and read the book but hadn't gotten around to sending her a message. And now it was too late.

I know this is a stupid thing to say, but I'm going to say it anyway. Sandra Saldanha was an unlikely victim of murder. She read books by Tolstoy and Dickens. She had a balcony full of thriving plants. She'd started a collection drive when the yoga teacher needed surgery. She was even friendly with the limp librarian.

Sandra Saldanha had been a nice person. Given that The Orchard by Kotecha is crawling with people who are not nice, it seemed wrong that she should have been the one who was murdered.

Even so, that is what happened.

On Tuesday morning, somebody rang Sandra Saldanha's doorbell and walked into her apartment.

There was a scuffle, a shriek, a determined shove. Then a frail body falling, falling, falling all the way from the 56th floor of Maple Towers into the swimming pool of The Orchard with a dreadful splash.

Every time I thought about that early morning splash, I felt a lurch of horror. Every time I spotted Sandra Saldanha's name in my phone contacts I felt a stab of sadness. I knew exactly what Sunidhi meant when she said she was haunted by the murder.

'Did you know Sandra Saldanha?' Darius Engineer asked Sunidhi, breaking the uneasy silence in my bedroom.

'A little, I guess,' Sunidhi shrugged. 'I'm in Maple Towers, so I would see her in the lift, or the lobby and she always chatted. My mum and she were in the same yoga class and were pretty friendly. But that's not why I'm suggesting that we investigate the murder. I just thought that it was the obvious crime to solve.'

What Sunidhi said made sense. Except.

'Hasn't the murder been solved?' I asked at the very same moment that Nihal uttered his first sentence of the day. 'Didn't the driver do it?'

Sunidhi shrugged again. 'That's what the police are saying but...'

'But?'

'I think the police are working on the case again,' Sunidhi said. 'They landed up yesterday to ask my mum questions about the yoga class and whether we'd noticed any strangers around. My mum got the feeling that they're not entirely convinced about the driver—'

'I don't think anyone is entirely convinced about the driver,' I cut in. 'It just felt wrong.'

'Nobody can be that stupid,' Darius Engineer agreed.

Sandra Saldanha's driver was a grey-haired man named Gajanan Shinde who lived in Dombivli. On Monday night, Sandra Saldanha had phoned him and asked him to get to Maple Towers a few minutes before 8 a.m. the next morning.

As the local trains were running late on Tuesday, Gajanan Shinde only got to Maple Towers at 8.08 a.m. He called Apartment 562 from the building intercom downstairs, but Sandra Saldanha didn't respond. He called again and again and finally decided to go upstairs and ring the doorbell.

Up to this point, the police and Gajanan Shinde agreed on the sequence of events. But from here the versions diverged.

This is what the police said had happened: Gajanan Shinde had rung Sandra Saldanha's doorbell at 8.14 a.m. Sandra Saldanha had answered the door. Maybe she had berated the driver for being late, maybe they had fought about something else. At any rate, Gajanan Shinde had marched into the apartment, grabbed his employer, flung her out of the balcony and then stood in the middle of the living room, pretending to be bewildered.

This is what Gajanan Shinde said had happened: He'd stood outside the apartment and had rung the doorbell twice. Sandra Saldanha hadn't opened the door, but he could hear voices and a muffled scream on the other side. Then, just as he was about to ring the doorbell for the third time, the door had been flung open and a person had rushed out, pushed him aside and charged towards the staircase. The person had left the door of No. 562 open, and after a few moments, Gajanan had stepped inside. 'I only went in to check that Madam was fine,' he told the police. 'I called out, but nobody answered.'

Whichever version was accurate, one fact remained unchanged. At exactly 8.17 a.m., Sandra Saldanha had plummeted from the plant-filled balcony of a tall, bean-shaped building in Parel.

By 8.18 a.m. she was dead.

There were two problems with the driver's story:

1) Gajanan Shinde was unable to describe the person who ran out of Sandra Saldanha's house. He had no idea if the person had been male or female, old or young. All he could say was that the person was wearing jeans and a black shirt. And that the person had no face.
2) The CCTV didn't catch anyone running down the staircase from the 56th floor of Maple Towers. It didn't catch anyone entering the lift on the 56th floor either.

There were two problems with the police's story as well:

1) Sandra Saldanha was a great traveller. Wherever she went, she bought fridge magnets and masks. The fridge magnets were arrayed on her Samsung fridge. The masks were displayed on a single wall in the living room.

   After the murder, the police and neighbours noticed that one mask—a flat, polished brown affair with two holes for eyes—was missing. The police decided that Gajanan had hidden it away to strengthen his story about the intruder without a face.

   But hidden it where? The mask had disappeared without a trace.

   (I knew some of this because Kavita maushi, who worked for Sandra Saldanha, lives three doors away from Jaishree didi, who cleans for us. Kavita maushi maintained that the mask had been on the wall on Monday and that she should know because she dusted every single mask every single day.)

2) The police couldn't find a motive. Gajanan Shinde had worked for Sandra Saldanha for nineteen years and they'd been fond of each other. This made it difficult to accept the police's hypothesis that Sandra Saldanha had yelled at

Gajanan for arriving late and that the driver had gotten so angry that he had murdered her.

'You know what bothers me the most?' Sunidhi asked as we discussed the Gajanan Shinde angle.

'What?'

'That there really wasn't time for such a terrible fight. Gajanan Shinde reached the 56th floor of Maple Towers at 8.13 a.m. It took another minute for him to ring the doorbell. The murder was committed at 8.17 a.m. Is three minutes enough time to have such an awful fight that it ends in murder? I honestly don't think so.'

I was about to agree, but the boys got there first. 'Great point,' Darius Engineer exclaimed, while Nihal Advani nodded and said, 'Yes.'

I bristled. Whenever I said anything, Darius Engineer snickered and did his 'Who let the dogs out woof woof' thing. And Nihal Advani did his turned-into-stone thing. But here they were, showering Sunidhi with praise and admiration.

Irritation made me combative. 'Maybe the newspapers got the timings wrong,' I challenged.

Sunidhi shook her head. 'The timings are right,' she said. 'I asked the security guards in Maple Towers. Tiwariji and Bhonsleji were on duty on Tuesday morning when Gajanan Shinde came in. Tiwariji is new so I don't know him well, but his daughter is studying to be a doctor. Bhonsleji has high blood pressure, and his son is not doing well in school. He helped me find my mobile phone a couple of months ago after I put it down to tie my shoelaces and then Adviti walked past so I started chatting and forgot to—'

'What did the security guards say?' I interrupted curtly. I didn't want to know more about Bhonsleji. And I really, really didn't want to know more about snooty Adviti Arora.

'Tiwariji said that the timings were accurate. He was around when...when...'

'When splash, smash, splatter,' Darius supplied so loudly that I jumped.

Sunidhi and I were glaring at Darius when Nihal surprised us by speaking. 'Three minutes is not enough time to have a fight that ends in murder,' he said. 'Which means that if the driver killed Sandra Saldanha, he planned it in advance. And if he planned it in advance, why would he do it so that he was the obvious suspect?'

One more question without an answer. If it was not Gajanan Shinde it was someone else—

'Wait a minute,' I gasped, trying to trap a thought that was scuttling around in my head. 'Let's assume that the killer was someone who landed up at Sandra Saldanha's house on Tuesday morning. Sandra Saldanha opened the door, and the killer entered her apartment. They talked for a bit and then the killer pushed her off the balcony.'

'Yaaaa yaaaa,' Darius said smirkily. 'We know all that already.'

I ignored Darius and said slowly, 'Just think about it. If we hadn't known that there was somebody else in the apartment when Sandra Saldanha fell from her balcony, what would we have thought?'

'That,' Sunidhi squeaked, 'that it was an accident.'

'Or,' Nihal said, sitting up ramrod straight, 'that she had committed suicide.'

The electric silence in the room was broken when Darius singsonged, 'But Perfect Paro is forgetting something. Anybody standing in a balcony of Banyan, Gulmohar or Cedar Towers could have seen what was going on in Sandra Saldanha's balcony. Which would make it risky to stage a suicide or an accident.'

I haven't yet mastered the art of raising a single eyebrow, so I made do with an eyeroll. 'I don't think you've seen Sandra Saldanha's balcony,' I singsonged right back before jumping up and leading the way to my own balcony.

Nihal and Sunidhi hurried behind me and although Darius dragged his feet, he did get there eventually.

The balcony of No. 492 juts out from the side of Banyan Towers like a semicircular shelf. When we looked down, we could see the pool, dazzlingly blue in the midday light. When we looked up, we could see the semi-circular balconies of the other Orchard buildings. Including the one from which a body had tumbled into the swimming pool just four days ago.

Identifying Sandra Saldanha's home on the 56th floor of Maple Towers was easy. While the other Maple Towers balconies featured cane chairs, glass-topped tables, grills and well-behaved potted plants, the balcony of No. 562 housed an unruly jungle. From where we stood, we could see large palms, a flowering frangipani, abundant ferns and twisty creepers, which together made an effective green screen.

'The killer must have known about the plants,' I said, pointing at the balcony and trying not to think about what had played out behind that leafy veil on Tuesday morning.

Standing next to me, Sunidhi was equally subdued. 'I think you're right,' she whispered. 'The killer was hoping to stage a suicide or an accident, but the plan got messed up because Gajanan Shinde was outside the door and ringing the doorbell.'

'The bloody killer must have pooped in his pants,' Darius crowed, forgetting to sulk in the excitement of the moment.

I wouldn't have used those words exactly, but Darius was right. 'The killer needed to get out of the apartment in a hurry,' I agreed. 'He or she grabbed a mask, wore it and rushed out. Then poor Gajanan Shinde walked into the apartment and became the obvious suspect.'

It was Nihal who spotted the single flaw in the theory. 'There's one problem,' he said.

‘Yes,’ I sighed, as we headed back to my bedroom, ‘the CCTV footage doesn’t show anyone besides Gajanan Shinde. So where did the killer go?’

Sunidhi looked crushed, but Darius laughed. ‘Those CCTV cameras are useless,’ he said.

‘What do you mean?’ Nihal asked.

‘There’s only one camera on each floor,’ Darius explained. ‘It only covers half the corridor. The service elevator and the part of the staircase that goes upwards are not covered by the camera at all. There are a hundred ways to avoid being caught. I’m the expert.’

‘The expert on avoiding CCTV cameras?’ Sunidhi goggled. ‘How come?’

Darius assumed an air of mystery, but I knew the answer. Avoiding the unblinking eye of a CCTV camera was an essential skill if you were a habitual slipper of threatening notes and ringer of doorbells in the middle of the night. It was a skill that Darius had clearly mastered. ‘The killer could have walked close to the wall and taken the service elevator up a couple of floors and then taken the regular elevator all the way down,’ he explained. ‘Or he—’

‘He or she,’ Sunidhi interrupted. ‘Why are you assuming that the killer is male?’

‘I thought women poison their victims or bore them to death,’ Darius guffawed and looked disappointed when we ignored him.

'Well, you know about the CCTV cameras because—' I paused, heroically resisting the temptation to list out Darius's past crimes, 'because you live here. But the killer is probably some outsider who's been to Maple Towers maybe two or three times. How would he or she know?'

'By checking in advance,' Darius shrugged. 'The killer must have taken a good look at the cameras and elevators and staircases before landing up to actually commit the murder.'

The idea of a person prowling around Maple Towers, checking the angles of CCTV cameras, and plotting the death of an old woman was, for some reason, more upsetting than the murder itself. 'This is sick,' Sunidhi wailed. 'Do you think we'll ever know the truth? I can't bear the thought that we might never find out.'

Once again, I knew what Sunidhi meant. The thought that Sandra Saldanha might have taken the truth to the grave with her was unbearable.

We needn't have worried. The dead have ways of communicating with the living.

Sandra Saldanha had already sent us a message. It was sitting in a blue backpack on the green armchair in my bedroom, waiting to be discovered. Within a couple of hours, the Chicken Pox Club would be in business.

An Intriguing Scrap of Paper

Saturday, May 6

Meena didi is one of those people who's always in a hurry, and who does things exactly thirty-five minutes before anyone else. So, of course, she summoned us for lunch at 12.25 p.m.

Darius, Sunidhi, Nihal and I obediently trooped to the dining table, sat down and served ourselves tomato soup and cheese-potato toasties. Maybe it was Meena didi's brisk presence. Maybe we were feeling ill. Or maybe we remembered that we were almost strangers. Whatever the reason, we lapsed into an awkward silence.

'Miss Rehana should be coming now,' I said, hoping the others would leave soon after.

'I've never met Miss Rehana,' Sunidhi piped up. 'Is she nice? Is she a detective?'

'She's got some fancy degree,' Darius sniggered. 'But she's female, so how can she be a detective?'

'So witty,' I snapped, unable to help myself.

'Ohh, the dogs are getting ready to bite,' Darius laughed and started woofing till I jumped up in red-faced irritation.

I'm not the sort of person who stabs people with forks but—as Miss Pavri keeps telling us in English Language class—there are exceptions to every rule. It was a good thing, then, that Sunidhi hurried to change the subject. 'We have to choose one mystery to investigate,' she said. 'Let's decide before Miss Rehana gets here.'

Taking a deep breath, I forced myself to calm down before asking, 'Aren't we focusing on the Sandra Saldanha murder?'

'Let's choose after we hear Nihal's mystery,' Sunidhi suggested.

'Does Nihal even have a mystery?' Darius scoffed.

Nihal dipped his toasty in ketchup, took a bite, chewed it for the recommended thirty-two times and drank a spoonful of soup before looking up and saying, 'Yes.'

'What?' I asked.

'It may be nothing,' Nihal said, eating methodically.

'But it may be something,' Sunidhi laughed. 'So you might as well tell us.'

'Okay,' Nihal said, getting up and heading to my bedroom.

He was back a moment later with his blue backpack. He placed the backpack on the living room sofa and unzipped a small side pocket. From there he took out a piece of grubby white paper, which he carefully unfolded on the dining table. It was quite a build-up and Darius, Sunidhi and I bent over the paper with eager eyes.

The sheet of paper was about the size of a Kindle. It was creased and smeared with what looked like mud. This is what was written on it:

> ***MOODY***
> *SC*
> *NW S 13?*
> *NE 6 A?*
> *N 10 J?*
> *Burst balloon*
> *Open book without words*
> *Rossetti*
> *Young man—train—Callian/Calian*

The MOODY had been written with a black marker pen in big block letters and circled with a heavy hand.

The SC had been underlined three or four times.

The jumble of letters and numbers had been scribbled in a haphazard manner, as if someone had been taking notes during a bumpy car trip.

The last three lines had been written in in a hasty scrawl.

We stared at the scribbles and turned to Nihal.

'What's this?'

'Is it some sort of code?'

'What book without words?'

'Who is Rossetti?'

'I don't know,' Nihal said, after our questions had dried up. 'I guess that's why it's a mystery.'

'We get that it's a mystery,' I replied. 'But why is it a mystery worth solving? It almost looks like someone has jotted down train seat numbers or chess moves or something. Why should we care?'

'Because of where it was found,' Nihal replied.

'And where was it found?' Darius asked, sounding as exasperated as I felt.

Nihal didn't reply. Instead, he returned to his blue backpack, unzipped another compartment, and pulled out a book. It was an old paperback with an olive green cover and a title written in fussy black lettering: *Poems of Strength and Comfort*.

We did some more staring till I finally asked, 'What's so special about this book?'

Again, Nihal didn't say anything. Instead, he turned the green cover to reveal the first page. Then he placed it on the table and waited while Darius, Sunidhi and I crowded around.

The first page of the book looked like the first page of any other book. It was blank, barring the title and the name of the owner written in the top right-hand corner in faded blue ink.

Someone choked. Someone else dropped a spoon. I found myself gulping as I stared at the two words inscribed in a flowing, loopy hand.

Sandra Saldanha.

Too Many Doorbells

Saturday, May 6

'Where did you get this book from? Did it belong to Sandra Saldanha?'

'Did she give it to you?'

'Is this a joke? Or is this serious?'

'What does it mean?'

Sunidhi, Darius and I were pelting Nihal with questions when the doorbell ding-donged.

The doorbell ding-donged as it always does. As all the doorbells of The Orchard by Kotecha ding-dong. But for some reason, we stiffened. We were all afraid of what stood on the other side.

The mangled, shattered corpse of an English professor. A killer without a face. Or, worse, a killer with a familiar face.

'It must be Miss Rehana,' Darius said, and we relaxed.

Of course, it was Miss Rehana. What were we even thinking?

When Meena didi opened the door, however, the person on the other side was not Miss Rehana. It was Dr Prabhu.

The doctor was smug about killing four birds with one stone. 'All together, all together,' he said, rubbing gleeful hands. 'So how are you? How are you? Any fever? Any cough? Any discomfort? Any fever? Eating healthy? Any itching?'

Dr Prabhu was careful to keep the table between himself and his contagious patients and I again wondered why someone so terrified of ordinary chicken pox had become a doctor. Looking up, I caught Sunidhi's eye. She began to giggle, and, for an alarming moment, I thought I was going to giggle along.

The moment passed and I informed the doctor that the four of us were moving from the papule stage to the pustule stage of chicken pox.

I was proud of my precise health report, but Dr Prabhu didn't acknowledge it. He was too busy staring slack-jawed at something on the table. At first, I thought he was gaping at the olive green book of poetry and the scrap of paper. But then I identified the culprit—the plastic poop that Darius had brought along to the dining table.

To be fair to Dr Prabhu, poop is not something you would expect to find on a dining table—especially if you didn't know that it was plastic. Much as I disliked the doctor, I couldn't blame him for turning grey-green and bidding us a hasty farewell.

'Same time...tomorrow...' he choked, backing away. 'I will see all of you here.'

'Doctor, we won't be here tomorrow,' Sunidhi said. 'It's Sunday so Darius, Nihal and I will be at home.'

'And I'm going to my Nani's for lunch,' I added.

Dr Prabhu stopped glaring at the table so that he could glare at us. 'I may not be able to do four visits on a Sunday,' he whined. 'I think you can all meet here for one hour.'

'That won't be possible,' I repeated, 'because I'm going to my Nani's house.'

Dr Prabhu glared even harder. 'You are leaving the premises?' he asked with an accusatory sniff.

'Yes,' I said. 'The building office has scheduled pest control treatment tomorrow morning. They're refusing to postpone it and I'm allergic to the spray so I can't stay at home.'

'But you will be infectious—'

'Everyone in my Nani's house has had chicken pox, so it's fine.'

'My advice is that you should stay at home,' Dr Prabhu said, pouting and looking like he was about to stamp his foot. 'This is very foolish.'

I wondered why Dr Prabhu was so agitated. Was he worried that my chicken pox would take a turn for the worse? I didn't think so.

Was he worried that I would infect the wider public? Once again, I didn't think so.

Was he cross that he would miss out on his fees for the day? Most likely, I decided.

I was not the only one to think so. As soon as the doctor departed in a haze of petulance, Nihal remarked, 'He just wants to see us together and bill us individually.'

When you got to know him, Nihal was not such a bland-tofu boy after all.

The encounter with Dr Prabhu perked us up. We spent a happy five minutes finishing the brownies that Sunidhi's mother had sent and laughing over the doctor's undoctorlike behaviour. For once Darius and I were in agreement and Nihal was almost chatty. 'He didn't look at our boils even once,' he remarked.

'He was staring at the food,' Sunidhi said. 'Maybe he was hungry.'

'No, no. He was staring at the plastic poop, and I don't blame him. Darius, can you please put that gross thing away. And Nihal, you still have to tell us about—' I was saying when the doorbell rang again.

Once again, we thought it was Miss Rehana. Once again it was not.

This time it was two strangers.

The first stranger was a man with a shiny purple-blue shirt, fleshy pink lips and straggly shoulder-length hair that was held back with a black plastic hairband.

The second stranger was a wiry man with a shaved head and tattoos on his arms. He was wearing a tight black T-shirt, track pants and a pious expression.

Both men seemed to think that they had every right to march through the door of No. 492 Banyan Towers. Well, I was about to correct their misconception.

'Yes?' I asked coldly. 'Do you need something?'

'I'm here to meet Mr Mehta,' the black T-shirt man announced, holding his hands up in a theatrical namaste.

'My father's gone to office,' I replied.

'But it is Saturday,' the man objected in a disbelieving voice and odd accent—the sort that an American actor might adopt when popping on a turban and playing the part of an Indian. 'I am Gurudev Mishr. I heard that Mr Mehta wants to start yoga class so I thought I will meet him today.'

I frowned. Why would my father want to do yoga with someone who looked like a bodyguard? For that matter, why would my father want to do yoga at all? Wasn't it enough that he ran, swam and played tennis?

'Who told you that my father wants to do yoga?' I asked, wondering if the man had landed up at the wrong apartment.

'Aarti Madam from the 11th floor,' the yoga teacher replied.

The 'Oh' that flew out of me was so sharp and hard that Sunidhi, Darius and Nihal turned to stare.

Aarti Madam from the 11th floor had that effect on me every time.

Aarti Butalia had moved into Banyan Towers with her brother about six months ago. She had moved into our lives a couple of months later, after meeting my father in the gym. Suddenly, she was everywhere—draped on the grey sofa in the living room in a too-tight black dress; inviting my father for coffee on random Tuesday nights; googling summer camps in France and Spain, 'which would be so good for Paro's life skills'. (She just wanted to get rid of me for three weeks or so. Well, I wanted to get rid of her for forever. And anyway, who said she could call me Paro?)

Aarti Butalia was attractive in an over-thin, over-lipsticked way. Her voice and mannerisms were as sweet as toffee—the cheap kind that sticks in your teeth and gives you cavities. It bothered me that I was the only one to sense the feral, grasping core beneath the sugar-coating. The only one to mind that while it was Aarti Butalia who suggested expensive meals and movies, it was my father who ended up paying for them. Every time. Not just for her, but for her rat-like brother as well.

Unless I acted swiftly and craftily, Aarti Butalia and her yoga mat would be parked in our living room every Sunday morning.

'My father hasn't said anything,' I said to the yoga teacher. 'Why don't you call him and fix an appointment?'

'I will come tomorrow,' Gurudev Mishr said. 'Tomorrow is Sunday.'

'We are having pest control done and we won't be at home,' I snapped. 'And my father is very busy. Best you call him after a month. Maybe two.'

I stared pointedly at the door, but the yoga teacher didn't take the hint. Instead, he nodded at his companion who sprang to life, marched up to Sunidhi and said, 'You haven't filled your feedback form.'

Sunidhi giggled and ducked her head. 'I'm sorry,' she said. 'I'll do it later today.'

'We've sent you three reminders,' Mr Purple Shirt snapped.

'I practise the Butterfly Leap every day,' Sunidhi replied. 'I think I've sort of got the first part, but you know the moment when you are supposed to—'

Mr Purple Shirt didn't look particularly interested in Sunidhi's progress with the Butterfly Leap. 'You didn't answer our messages,' he cut in. 'Miss Heena sent so many messages.'

'I have a procrastination problem,' Sunidhi explained cheerfully. 'I've even been to a therapist for it. But today, promise.'

Mr Purple Shirt was having none of it. He stalked up to the dining table and thrust a form at Sunidhi, saying with a reproachful sigh, 'Up and down, up and down I have been going looking for you.'

Given that he had been going up and down, up and down in the supersonic elevators of The Orchard by Kotecha there really was no reason for him to look so aggrieved. I glanced at Sunidhi and, noticing her expression, felt a giggle bubble up. (This was a habit I needed to squash.)

'Sorry, Renato Sir,' Sunidhi said, looking anything but sorry. 'I'll fill the form now.'

Renato Sir. So this was the dance teacher who couldn't dance.

Unlike the yoga teacher who didn't look like a yoga teacher, Renato Sir looked like a Renato Sir. I gazed at him with interest while he continued to speak in a breathless, peevish manner. 'We need it for our records. We need you to write that you stopped the class for health reasons. Not because of anything the dance instructors did. We don't want any problems later.'

Sunidhi got to work. The form was six pages long and Sunidhi was an earnest filler of forms, which gave our unwelcome visitors plenty of time to make themselves at home.

Renato Sir asked for a glass of water.

The yoga teacher asked for a piece of paper so that he could write a note for my father. Then he walked up to the table and spotted the plastic poop. His sharp intake of breath alerted Renato Sir to the fact that something was off. So then Renato Sir looked at the table, spotted the plastic poop and choked.

Great. By evening, every single person in The Orchard by Kotecha would be whispering that Paromita Mehta served poop for lunch.

The moment our uninvited visitors left, I snarled at Darius, 'Put that thing away. It's scarred Dr Prabhu, that Renato man and that yoga teacher for life. It's disgusting.'

Darius looked mutinous and started droning 'Who let the dogs out'. I was about to argue, when our overworked doorbell rang once again.

This time it was Miss Rehana.

Miss Rehana is twenty-seven years old and pretty in a serious, bespectacled way. She wears chunky silver jewellery, block print kurtas and ties her hair in a long plait. Although she studied in the UK and returned to India last year, she still doesn't have a proper job. Which is why she's working part-time for two detective agencies and conducting The Clue Crew workshop.

Miss Rehana came into the living room looking flustered. 'Sorry, I'm late. Prakash Sir is unwell and can't give his talk on Monday. So, I had to let all the parents know and I had to plan an activity for Monday. I won't be able to stay too long but I thought I would meet you for ten minutes.'

The news about Prakash Talwar cheered me up. 'Will he be giving his talk later?' I asked eagerly. 'Do you think you can fix it after five or six days so that we can also attend?'

'Let's see,' Miss Rehana said with the vague smile that adults stick on their faces when they're unable to say 'yes' but don't want to say 'no'. 'But for now, why don't you quickly tell me about your mysteries?'

We made our way to my bedroom, where we sat in a circle on the blue rug. Miss Rehana read my newspaper clipping. Then she examined Darius's squished metal object and said it looked more like a nail than a bullet. Next, she listened to Sunidhi's idea and agreed that Gajanan Shinde was an unlikely killer.

'Let's see what the police do,' she said. 'They usually know more than they say.'

It was when Miss Rehana saw Nihal's offering that she shed her distracted air. 'Where did you find this?' she asked Nihal. 'What do all these numbers and letters mean? Did this book really belong to Sandra Saldanha?'

Nihal took a sip of water from his metal bottle and screwed the top back on. Then he told us the story behind the grubby scrap of paper.

Nihal Advani loved books. When his mother realized he had chicken pox and that he would be stuck at home, she hurried to The Orchard library.

The limp-wristed librarian had called in sick, so Mrs Advani wandered around without supervision. She looked through the shelf labelled 'Children 13 to 16' and chose a couple of Alex Riders. Then—because she was going to be in Bangalore over the weekend and wanted to keep Nihal busy—she continued to look around till she spotted a battered copy of *The Scarlet Pimpernel* on the librarian's table.

The book under *The Scarlet Pimpernel* was called *The Brontesaurus* and Mrs Advani assumed that it was about dinosaurs. She further assumed that the stack of books had been returned by a child around Nihal's age. As she was in a huge hurry, she grabbed the entire pile, took a quick picture and WhatsApped it to the librarian along with the message: 'Books I am borrowing. Advani. 341 Gulmohar Towers'.

Then she rushed back home, dumped the books on Nihal's bed and charged off to catch her flight.

All this took place on Friday morning while Nihal was in my bedroom, attending the first meeting of the Detective Club. When he got home, he looked through the pile and put aside the Alex Riders because he'd read them twice. Then he examined *The Scarlet Pimpernel* and decided that it looked promising—which was more than he could say about the remaining books.

The Brontesaurus was about those Brontë sisters—the ones who'd written those morbid books about orphan girls and doomed love that Nihal was never going to read.

Another was about yoga.

A third was a collection of poems about strength and courage.

The last one was called A *Comprehensive Dictionary of Diseases*.

What on earth had his mother been thinking? Nihal picked up his phone and typed out a terse message. 'Why have you brought me books about death and diseases? Are you trying to make me feel worse?' And then, because he was mad at his mother for going off to Bangalore when he was sick, he sent her pictures of random pages from the books.

A paragraph on the benefits of bhujanga asana. (Helps to soothe sciatica. Improves blood circulation...)

Then two pages dedicated to diseases starting with H that had been flagged by a square of pink paper. (Haemophilia, Hand-Foot-and-Mouth Disease, Hantavirus, Hepatitis A.)

Then a verse from a poem that went:

> Beyond this place of wrath and tears
> Looms but the Horror of the shade,
> And yet the menace of the years
> Finds and shall find me unafraid

Nihal was leafing through the doleful poems, looking for yet another nugget for his mother when he happened to turn to the first page. And realized that the book of poems was not so dull after all.

Written in the top right corner in a long-ago blue pen was the name 'Sandra Saldanha'. All it took were those two words to transform the book into an object of dark fascination.

Nihal leafed through the book of poetry page by page, which was when he made his second discovery. A mud-stained slip of paper tucked between two poems of strength and courage.

The poem on page 116 was called 'Do not stand at my grave and weep', and the name said it all. The poem on page 117 was called 'Remember' and was not much better.

Could Sandra Saldanha have foreseen her death? Nihal was so unsettled by the idea that he almost overlooked the makeshift bookmark. But the mud stains intrigued him.

Sandra Saldanha had been a professor of English who valued books. It seemed odd that she should use a dirty scrap of paper as a bookmark. Suddenly curious, Nihal unfolded the paper and stared at the urgent, untidy scrawls. Then he asked himself the obvious question: Could this chit of paper be linked to the murder that had stunned the city three days ago?

After which he supplied himself with the obvious answer: Probably not.

The words on the muddy chit could have been written by someone else. Or they could have been written by Sandra Saldanha at any point over the past five decades.

Nihal had just about convinced himself of this when he flipped the paper around and noticed two things.

That somebody had sketched something that looked like a pillar draped with a garland of flowers. And that this scrap of paper had begun life as a bill.

The bill had been written by a Samsung technician who had replaced components in Sandra Saldanha's washing machine. The technician had written three lines about electric circuits, pipes, and ball bearings. Nihal barely noticed those details. He was too busy staring at the date scrawled at the top.

Saturday, 29 April 2023.

Sandra Saldanha had died on 2 May 2023.

The Samsung technician had visited Sandra Saldanha three days before she tumbled out of her balcony. Which meant that sometime during the last seventy-two hours of her life, Sandra Saldanha had jotted a jumble of numbers, letters and random words on the back of a bill.

What did they mean? How had Sandra Saldanha gotten mud all over the bill? Why had she tucked it into a book between two grim poems about death?

'The questions bothered me,' Nihal explained in his unemphatic way. 'I thought it might be worth investigating.'

His audience, sitting cross-legged and still on the blue rug, nodded in rapt agreement.

We Get Down to Sleuthing

Monday, May 8

It was 2.30 p.m. by the time we got the story out of Nihal Advani. Miss Rehana had forgotten that she was in a hurry. I had forgotten that I wanted my bedroom to myself. And Nihal had forgotten that he didn't talk.

We examined the scribbles on the back of the grubby bill and wondered aloud. MOODY? NE 6 A? Burst balloon? What could they possibly mean?

Only one word on the list made sense—and I'm proud to say that it was I who made the connection. (All thanks to Miss Pavri, my English teacher. And so indirectly thanks to Sandra Saldanha, who had been her English teacher. Which is a goosebumps-inducing thought.)

I'd been wondering if NE 6 A was connected to a crossword puzzle when my eyes fell on the word 'Rossetti'. It felt vaguely familiar, and I was wondering if Rossetti was a clothes brand when a wispy memory floated by. A memory of Miss Pavri teaching us an

Elizabeth Barrett Browning sonnet a few months ago. (The one I'd analyzed in the test and topped with 18 on 20.)

Miss Pavri had also told us about the other poets of that period and read out their works. One of them had been a doleful poem about death which, for some reason, was linked in my head with the word 'Rossetti'.

A sudden idea made me sit up.

'Nihal,' I asked abruptly, 'where exactly was the paper? Between which two poems?'

Nihal picked up *Poems of Strength and Courage*, opened it to the relevant page and handed the book to me. The poem on Page 116 was 'Do not stand at my grave and weep' and had been written by someone called Mary Frye.

The poem on Page 117 was called 'Remember' and had been written by Christina Rossetti.

'Look,' I squawked, almost incoherent with excitement. 'Rossetti.'

Sunidhi was the first person to get it. 'Oh wow, oh wow,' she yelped even louder than me. 'So the paper was not just shoved between the random pages of a random book. There's a proper link between the scribbles and the poem. It means something.'

Of course, Darius was quick to pop the bubble of our excitement. 'I bet it's some silly literature quiz,' he said. 'I can't think of a single way that this stupid poem is connected with the murder.'

To be honest, neither could I. Not even after Sunidhi read the poem out in an inappropriately bouncy voice.

'Remember me when I am gone away,
Gone far away into the silent land;
When you can no more hold me by the hand,
Nor I half turn to go yet turning stay...'

'What does all this mean?' I asked when Sunidhi was done. 'What is this all about?'

The answer came from an unexpected source.

'Death,' Nihal said. 'This is all about death.'

The creepy pronouncement darkened the mood, and we were grateful when Miss Rehana took charge. 'Let's start with some basic investigation,' she said. 'By Monday morning, we should try and have a better idea about Sandra Saldanha, her life and her death. We should also make a list of people who knew her and can tell us about her activities and state of mind during the last week of her life. Was she scared? Or upset about anything? Had she had a fight with anyone? The police will have covered that, but you never know. Paromita, make a list of who will do what.'

Ten minutes later, I posted a 'List of Tasks to be completed by Monday morning' on the Detective Club chat:

Nihal

1) Find out how SS's book landed up in library
2) Read news reports about murder. Any new details?

Sunidhi

1) Talk to Maple Towers security to find out if they know anything else
2) Ask mother about SS's mood and behaviour during last few yoga classes

Darius

1) Check the CCTV camera on the 56th floor of Maple Towers and see if easy to avoid
2) Ask Mr Khurana—neighbour and former policeman—if he can identify code

Paromita

1) Find background on SS, interests, family, life
2) Find people who might know about her movements during last week of life

Miss Rehana

Ask senior detectives if they can identify code

Once the list was in place, Miss Rehana booked her Uber. 'What are we doing with the paper?' she asked as she picked up her embroidered bag. 'We should put it somewhere safe. Nihal maybe—'

'I'll keep it,' I cut in. 'Better it isn't moved from one place to another.'

'Okay,' Miss Rehana agreed. 'So long as you're careful.'

'Of course,' I responded in a prim tone that indicated that I was always careful.

I smoothed out the creased sheet, placed it in the front right-hand corner of my dressing table drawer and put the brown ceramic cow from Switzerland on it as a paperweight.

Darius Engineer, who has the wit of a warthog, found this hilarious. He started calling me Paranoid Paromita, Paraparo and similar. 'Who,' he chortled, 'will be interested in a messy piece of paper on which Sandra Saldanha wrote train seat numbers?'

Miss Rehana shrugged. 'There's a 99 per cent chance that you're right,' she said. 'But there's that 1 per cent chance that you're wrong. So best to be careful.'

Darius made scoffing sounds, but the rest of us nodded solemnly.

'Should we tell the police about the book and the piece of paper?' Sunidhi asked.

'Let's wait for a few days,' Miss Rehana said. 'Let's see what you uncover and then decide. Let me also ask Prakash Sir, Reena Ma'am and Girish Sir. They will know what to do.'

'It's too exciting that we are in the middle of a real case,' Sunidhi said, somehow managing to bounce in the cross-legged position.

'Let's see what happens,' Miss Rehana laughed. 'Are you guys meeting tomorrow?'

'I wish we were,' Sunidhi sighed. 'But my family has a Sunday-is-for-the-family obsession.'

‘And I have to go to my Nani’s house,’ I added, ‘because the pest control people are landing up here.’

‘I’ll see you on Monday then,’ Miss Rehana said, waving and hurrying out of the door.

The others left soon after and I spent the rest of the evening dipping into *The Good Girl’s Guide to Murder*, drinking Duke’s Lemonade and dozing fitfully till bedtime.

Big Gains, Bigger Losses

Sunday, May 7

I devoted Sunday morning to getting to know Sandra Saldanha better.

The English professor may not have been a celebrity, but she'd written books, won awards and taught thousands of students (including two Bollywood actors, one bigshot surgeon, three well-known journalists and a bunch of rich bankers and industrialists). The newspapers had interviewed her students and colleagues and carried long pieces about Sandra Saldanha's life and death.

I read the articles on my computer and made notes in an unused HDFC Bank diary. I soon had four pages filled with basic information:

Background

- Born in 1960
- Grew up in Santa Cruz
- Youngest of three siblings. Both brothers dead.
- Brilliant student. After graduating from St Paul's College, went on to study at Cambridge.

- Returned to India some years later and taught at St Paul's College for thirty-three years
- Retired from St Paul's two years ago
- Wrote four books—two biographies, one book of non-fiction and one book of poetry

Family

- Never married
- Closest relative is nephew Donny Saldanha in Melbourne
- Donny says he was very fond of Aunty Sandra, but he last met her six years ago and last spoke to her in February when she called on his birthday
- Likely that Donny will inherit Sandra Saldanha's money and apartment in Maple Towers

Interests and personality

- Kind, intelligent, caring, feisty (People always say good things about the dead, but here the affection seemed genuine.)
- All agree that Sandra Saldanha didn't just care about her students' academic performance, she cared about their happiness. Many stories about how she drove students to hospital; how she spent hours helping them choose the right career path; and how she held extra classes for struggling students
- Had famously green thumb
- Committed to yoga

Once I was done with the recent articles, I started poking around on the Internet for older information. I hadn't expected much, which is why I ended up feeling like an archaeologist who digs for a single shard and comes up with a stash of coins, beads, bones, and utensils.

This is what I found:

- Two academic papers that Sandra Saldanha had written about famous Indian authors
- An interview in *Mid-Day* after one of her books was published
- A fortnightly column that she had written for an evening newspaper around ten years ago. The topics hopped all over the place—from sparrows to the history of the jalebi to caring for ferns in a Mumbai balcony.
- A loving piece she had written about St Paul's when the college turned 150 years old
- A chilling article about two students—both boys, both around twenty—who had caught a train to Kasara Station, gone for a trek in the hills and never returned. (The two boys disappeared on a rainy weekend in 1997. Sandra Saldanha wrote her article for *The Times* exactly two years later, in August 1999. The article gave me the shivers and I hoped the mystery had been solved.)
- Sandra Saldanha's book of poems, which had an eerily prophetic name. It was called *The View*

from a High Window. (A Kindle edition was available for Rs 175 and I almost bought it, but then had second thoughts. There was no way that a book of poetry could provide a clue for a crime committed fifteen years after it was published.)

- Three blog posts about trees and mangroves being destroyed in Mumbai. In these posts, Sandra Saldanha had named and shamed a bunch of evil builders (including our very own Mr Kotecha, who had apparently chopped down a real-life grove of banyan and peepal trees while constructing a complex called The Grove by Kotecha in Thane.)

This was the point at which I stopped googling and started thinking.

Mr Kotecha is a major figure in our world. His name appears on our postal address. His cars are always blocking our driveway. His daughter's wedding has driven us nuts over the last month. (Gauri Kotecha's wedding is an ongoing nightmare for The Orchard. Her endless functions are being held on the West Lawn, which means the joggers have nowhere to jog, and the walkers have nowhere to walk, and the children have nowhere to play hopscotch and cricket. We're constantly being stopped by gun-toting security men who act like we want to assassinate a VIP guest or two. Maple Towers is right next to the West Lawn, and the people living there look like sleep-deprived zombies thanks to the zillion-decibel music, screechy loudspeaker announcements and midnight drilling and stage-erecting.)

By now you've probably guessed that Mr Kotecha is not a wholesome individual. Even so, I couldn't see him sneaking out of his triple-decker penthouse, creeping down the staircase, crawling on all fours to avoid the CCTV cameras and throwing Sandra Saldanha out of her balcony because she called him 'a hypocrite' and 'an enemy of the environment' five months ago.

Still, I opened the HDFC diary and used a fluorescent orange pen to write the words 'Chief Suspects' on a blank page. Beneath that I wrote:

1) Mr Kotecha
2) Donny Saldanha

(Donny Saldanha made it to the list, not because I thought that he had flown down from Australia with a fake passport and murdered his aunt, but because *The Detective's Bible* insists that 'the heir to the fortune must be investigated'.)

Staring at this skimpy list, I felt discouraged.

How did it help to know that Sandra Saldanha had written a poem called 'Faces on a Passing Bus'? Or that she watered her ferns twice a day? What we really needed was to find her friends—the people she phoned when she was worried or confused. The people to whom she could say, 'There's something really bothering me, and it's to do with Rossetti and a burst balloon.'

These friends had to be out there somewhere, but how could we locate them?

Miss Pavri might know, but I could hardly message my English teacher in the middle of the summer holidays and ask her peculiar questions about her murdered English teacher. There were some boundaries I simply could not cross.

Feeling restless, I wandered into the kitchen for a glass of water and a Brazilnut biscuit. My father was in the living room, doing his Sunday morning thing—vacuuming up endless cups of ginger tea, reading his way through a stack of newspapers and tutting about interest rate hikes or whatever.

'Nothing but bad news,' he said, rustling the pages of *The Express*. 'Violence in Manipur. Shooting in a mall in Texas. They're predicting a very hot summer here. And there's one more article about that poor woman who was thrown into our swimming pool.'

'Sandra Saldanha?' I asked.

'Yes, yes. How many people do you know who are thrown into The Orchard swimming pool?'

Laughing, I peered over my father's shoulder and started reading the article beneath a headline that stated, 'Friends and colleagues mourn murdered teacher':

Friends, colleagues and former students described the 'glowing spirit' that made Sandra Saldanha, the English professor who was murdered on Tuesday morning, such a beloved teacher. At a prayer meeting held at St Paul's College, they shared memories about her life and sorrow over her brutal death.

'She encouraged us to dream,' said Rohit Kapasi, Bollywood heartthrob, after reciting a moving Urdu couplet. 'I find it difficult to come to terms with her death.'

This sentiment was echoed throughout the evening.

'Sandra, Danielle, Vidya and I met almost every single Saturday at The Gymkhana over the last thirty-five years,' said renowned sculptor Zarine Bhavnagri. 'We knew the ups and downs, the little joys and great sorrows of each other's lives. We knew when one of us was trying out a new recipe or was planning to buy a new computer. Sandra's passing has left a gaping hole in our lives.'

If I had been my Nani, I would have snapped my fingers and said, 'Bingo.'

If I had been Darius Engineer, I would have pumped my fist and said 'Yessss.'

As it is, I carried the newspaper to my bedroom, read the article twice and returned to Google. Ten minutes later, I knew that Zarine Bhavnagri was a well-known sculptor who had been at Cambridge with Sandra Saldanha.

That Vidya was Vidya Bhave, a former botany professor at St Paul's College. She was now part of the 'Save the Mangroves Foundation' and an expert on the native flora of Mumbai.

That Danielle was Danielle Vaz. Like Sandra Saldanha, she had taught English at St Paul's College. Unlike Sandra Saldanha, she was a controversial, flamboyant figure who had starred in numerous scandals. She had had an affair with a married painter, written a book that had been banned, had had a public fight with the Mumbai University vice chancellor.

I didn't know if Sandra Saldanha had met her friends on the last Saturday of her life. Or if she'd spoken to them about a poem by Christina Rossetti or a burst balloon. But I knew—without knowing how I knew—that Zarine, Danielle and Vidya would have answers.

Once again, I turned to Google. And once again Google delivered. It told me that Zarine Bhavnagri had a studio in an old mill compound, just ten minutes away from The Orchard by Kotecha. It also provided a phone number for the studio. (How on earth did detectives manage in the days before the Internet?)

I itched to call the studio, but it was Sunday, the studio was probably closed, and what would I say anyway? 'Hello Ms Bhavnagri. I am Paromita Mehta, a resident of The Orchard by Kotecha and a member of the Chicken Pox Club. We feel that the police might have made a mistake while investigating the death of Sandra

Saldanha. We are conducting a parallel investigation and would like to know if—just before dying—your friend happened to mention a book without words or a burst balloon or something called calian.'

In the best-case scenario, Zarine Bhavnagri would think I was a harmless lunatic. In the worst-case scenario, she would think I was the dangerous lunatic who had killed her best friend.

I was copying Zarine Bhavnagri's phone number into my notebook when the pest control people arrived with sprays, drills, and instructions. My father told me to wear a sweatshirt to conceal my scabs and then drove me to World Towers, where I spent the next three hours telling my Nani about the Chicken Pox Club and devouring a mango feast. Aam panna, aamras and puri, mango ice cream, two vegetables cooked with raw mango. Even the daal had been flavoured with the mango seed.

'This is my favourite meal of the year,' I told Nani, who looked delighted.

'Mango always used to make your mother sick,' she remarked, as she did every single summer. 'But you are like me, a mango girl. Take the ice cream home. You can share it with your new friends. And if you need a seventy-year-old detective, I would love to help. I read many Miss Marple books when I was young.'

At around 3 p.m., my father, a Tupperware box full of mango ice cream, a tall bottle of aam panna and I entered an apartment reeking with fumes and rattling with Meena didi's irritation.

'The pest control people found white ants in the storeroom,' Meena didi announced as soon as we stepped inside. 'They have drilled holes everywhere. They made me empty two cupboards and move everything in the kitchen. Then the supervisor came to check, and he hurt himself and had to sit down and put ice on the cut. Then the white ants men left, and the ants and cockroach men came, and they made me open all the cupboards and drawers so they could apply gel. They kept making me sign things and fill forms.'

'They've sprayed the whole house?' my father asked.

'I didn't let them do Paromita's room, which made the supervisor angry. Everything else is in a mess. And I haven't had a chance to clear up because people just kept coming. Three Amazon deliveries. Then that doctor. Then those two men from yesterday. And the bald one was trying to sit in the middle of the room with his eyes closed. Then Aarti madam's brother, then Aarti madam...I've been running the whole time.'

I hurried towards my bedroom to escape the chemical air and Meena didi's wrath but was unsuccessful. 'Paromita, why did you tell Dr Prabhu to come today?' Meena didi scolded. 'He was so insulted that you had gone out.'

‘I told Dr Prabhu *not* to come,’ I protested, but Meena didi continued to grumble till my father suggested she take the evening off.

Back in my bedroom, I spent a happy hour finishing *A Good Girl’s Guide to Murder*. After which I turned my attention to the murder in our swimming pool and decided to take another look at the muddy scrap of paper.

You already know what happened next. The scrap of paper was gone.

The missing scrap of paper upset me for many reasons.

Firstly, detectives are meant to find clues, not lose them.

Secondly, I’d acted all lofty with the other members of the Detective Club. I’d made it clear that I had better sleuthing skills. That I was more careful, more organized, more capable than they were. After which I’d promptly gone and lost our only clue. The others were bound to sneer. I would’ve sneered in their place.

Thirdly, as the minutes ticked on and the paper refused to surface, I started to think unpleasant thoughts. These turned even more unpleasant as Apartment No. 492 emptied out for the evening.

First Meena didi left to visit her sister in Bhayander. Then my father left to have drinks with ‘a friend’.

‘You’ll be fine, right?’ he asked as he always does.

'Obviously I will,' I replied as I always do. But this time it was untrue.

On this bruised, purple Sunday evening I didn't feel fine. I was convinced that something wicked was coming this way.

I peeped into the kitchen to make sure that it was empty of crazed killers. I avoided looking out of the window because I didn't want to see Sandra Saldanha's dark balcony, full of plants that had begun to wither and droop. I daren't play music or watch Netflix because I wanted to be alert to footsteps, rattling doors, creaking cupboards.

For the first time I realized that our light-hearted investigation was taking us to a very dark place.

A Growing List of Suspects

Monday, May 8

Sunidhi arrived at 9.57 a.m. on Monday morning. She was carrying a huge box of macaroons and wearing an even huger smile.

'I like your T-shirt. It looks very effortless. Effortless is so in,' she said, as she took off her Nikes and socks near the door. 'Have you found anything interesting? I've found all kinds of stuff. I'm not sure what's useful and what's not. Like, is it relevant that Sandra Saldanha had a peanut allergy? Or that she had a tiff with the new yoga teacher—the same guy who landed up on Saturday to meet your dad? Or that she was worried that she was overwatering her frangipani tree?'

'I don't know,' I said, reeling from the avalanche of information.

'I almost called you last evening to chat, but I thought you might be busy.'

'I almost called you last evening too,' I exclaimed. 'I've also found out a few things, but something awful has happened. The clue has—'

I was frantic to get my confession out of the way but before I could blurt it out, Nihal and Darius arrived with party packs of nachos and doughnuts. 'My mother sent these for breakfast,' Nihal said as he opened the Krispy Kreme box to reveal a dozen doughnuts, each in a different flavour.

Picking the right doughnut is serious business. We crowded around the box, and I reached out for one of those pillowy ones that's filled with custard and dipped in chocolate. Darius opted for a raspberry-filled doughnut and Nihal took one with a plain glaze. Sunidhi changed her mind about six times, but finally settled on a doughnut with yellow icing and sprinklies (but only after we assured her that she could have the one with the pink icing and sprinklies during the next round).

'Too sweet of your mom,' she told Nihal as she took her first bite. 'Too funny. It's like every single one of our moms woke up today and decided to give us a treat.'

The moment the words left her mouth, Sunidhi froze. The glance she threw at me was dismayed. In the embarrassed silence that followed, I wanted to say that it was okay. That they could talk about their mothers, even if I didn't have one. That my mum had been gone so long that I only missed her sometimes. That I had my dad and my Nani. And, on a good day, I also had Meena didi.

I could have said all this to Sunidhi. Even to Nihal. But not to Darius Engineer. I was afraid that he would ask a difficult question or crack a vile joke. So instead, I filled the mortified hush by saying in a rough voice, 'There's something I have to tell you.'

'What?' Sunidhi asked, alarmed. 'Has something happened?'

'Yes,' I said. 'I'm sorry. I honestly don't know how...I have no idea...'

'Paromita,' Nihal said quietly, 'just tell us.'

'Okay,' I sighed and then, dropping my hard voice and truculent pose, I broke the bad news. 'The clue... the paper that Nihal found...it's disappeared.'

Three faces gaped at me.

'Disappeared,' Sunidhi repeated blankly.

'How?' Nihal asked.

'You left it lying around and your maid threw it in the bin?' Darius cackled. 'Paranoid Paromita was careless?'

'Of course not,' I retorted. 'The paper was in my dressing table drawer the whole time. Then last evening I thought I would try to figure it out, but when I opened the dressing table drawer it was gone.'

'But how? You even put a paperweight on it,' Sunidhi said. 'It could hardly have flown away.'

'It definitely didn't fly away,' I agreed. 'I know that because the cow's left ear has gotten chipped, as if somebody moved it in a hurry and banged it on the side of the drawer.'

My words unleashed a barrage of exclamations.

'Are you serious?'

'Do you mean...'

'I don't know what to think,' I said. 'But I'm wondering if somebody took it.'

'Are you sure?' Darius asked in his rude way. 'It's difficult to believe.'

'Come and see,' I suggested, leading the way to my bedroom, and pulling the dressing table drawer open.

This time there were no surprises. The ceramic cow was still in the corner, looking wonky and wounded. The jewellery box, the Nivea cream, and the bag of scrunchies were still where they were supposed to be. The scrap of paper was still missing.

Sunidhi, Nihal and Darius stared and rummaged, just as I had done yesterday. Then they arrived at the same conclusion that I had arrived at yesterday.

'The only way it could have disappeared is if someone took it,' Darius said, peering inside the drawer and pointing to a small patch that was darker than the rest of the wood. 'Is this blood?'

'It could be,' Sunidhi exclaimed. 'The broken cow could have scratched the thief. What fun! This is so exciting. I'm actually happy I got chicken pox. So much better than doing dance with that bossy Miss Heena and being told that my legs are too short. It's even better than hanging out in the mall. Don't you think, Paromita?'

'Anything is better than the mall,' Darius said. 'Even spending a day looking for a scrap of paper.'

'Agree,' Nihal said, laughing.

Listening to them, it struck me that none of the others were particularly mad or sneery about the lost paper. If anything, they were sympathetic.

'You must have been so upset when you couldn't find the paper,' Sunidhi said.

'I was,' I admitted. 'I was alone last evening and kept imagining that the thief was still hiding in the house.'

The others looked startled. 'Paromita,' Sunidhi exclaimed, 'why didn't you just phone me? Naturally you were afraid. Because if someone took all the trouble to sneak into your apartment and steal the paper then...'

Sunidhi trailed off, but Nihal completed her sentence. 'Then there's a chance that the paper is connected to the murder.'

'And that the person who came here was the killer,' Darius added with relish.

I'd worked this out for myself, of course. Just as I'd asked myself the same questions that were now being hurled at me: Who had come into the apartment over the weekend? Who knew that we had the paper? Could Dr Prabhu have seen it when he came for a visit on Saturday? Or that dance teacher and that yoga teacher?

It was to find answers to these questions that I had staggered out of bed at the crack of dawn, as soon as Meena didi had begun clattering around the kitchen.

'Hi Meena didi,' I'd said in the most caring-sharing voice I could muster. 'Is your headache better? You must have gone nuts yesterday dealing with so many people. Do you remember all the people who landed up?'

Meena didi had thrown me a suspicious look. 'Why suddenly?' she'd asked in rapid-fire Marathi. 'You weren't interested yesterday.'

There was no way that I could concoct an elaborate lie at 7.12 a.m. And anyway, Meena didi was born with an in-built lie detector. So I'd stuck to the truth and told Meena didi that an important piece of paper had gone missing from my dressing table drawer. I was wondering if someone had snuck into my bedroom, stolen it and chipped the cow in the process.

Meena didi had been more concerned about the cow than the paper. 'Who would steal a scrap of paper?' she'd pooh-poohed. 'Is it the map to Shivaji's treasures or something?'

Once again, I'd stuck to the truth and explained that while the paper was unlikely to lead to Shivaji's treasures, it could lead to Sandra Saldanha's killer. Then—because this didn't sound very convincing—I'd told her about our investigations.

Meena didi loves Amazon Prime serials featuring blood-dripping knives and menacing shadows. Also, she hates having me underfoot because I disrupt her make-breakfast-air-the-living-room-water-the-plants rhythm. So, although she rolled her eyes and muttered—'You children are only doing time-pass'—she did answer my questions.

Which is how I, in turn, could answer Sunidhi, Darius and Nihal's questions.

'I was out on Sunday for about four hours and a whole bunch of people landed up just then,' I explained, before opening the HDFC diary and displaying the colour-coordinated chart which held information about those busy hours.

The chart caused a stir. Sunidhi admired my handwriting and ability to draw parallel lines. Darius was convinced that I was a weirdo. And Nihal grinned and asked, 'Don't they call you Meht-iculous in school? Now I know why.'

Darius started to hoot and gibber, but I spoke over his warthoggish babble. 'It was a mad morning so Meena didi might have confused a few details, but this is how she remembers it.'

Then I launched into the tidiest possible account of that chaotic Sunday morning:

- First, the pest control people.

  Two men to check for termites.

  Then their supervisor to get some forms signed.

  Then two men to spray the house for ants and cockroaches.

  Meena didi was sure the pest control people had been legit. They'd worn black uniforms and had documents that needed signing. They were going from apartment to apartment with sprays and drills.

The men in black had wandered all over the house. One of them could have stolen the paper, but the sequence of events was wrong. The pest control treatment had been scheduled a month ago—ages before Sandra Saldanha was murdered and a scrap of muddy paper landed up in my dressing table drawer.

I couldn't see how they could possibly be connected.

Conclusion: Not suspicious.

(Darius was attached to the idea that the killer had disguised himself as an employee of Pest O Kill and gained access to my bedroom. But how would a random killer know about the pest control treatment at our place? And wouldn't the other Pest O Kill people have objected if an unknown man popped up in their midst, just so he could lurk around the bedrooms of No. 492 Banyan Towers?)

- Then the three Amazon delivery men.

  The first had brought a Lotus Biscoff spread (For me).

  The second had brought shaving cream and an electric kettle (For my father and Meena didi respectively).

The third had delivered a bag of Cranberry Almond Millet Muesli.

(This had made me grit my teeth. Not because I dislike cranberries or almonds or even millets, but because the muesli had almost certainly been suggested by Aarti Butalia. She's one of those people who uses words like 'organic' and 'artisanal' and 'hand baked' at least two hundred times in a three-minute conversation. The first time she mentioned a 'hand-baked, gluten-free cake', I had remarked that I didn't know that there were people who baked with their feet. Aarti Butalia had tinkled and said that I had a wonderful sense of humour, but there was something cold and glinty in her eyes. The very next day she had asked my father why he wasn't sending me to boarding school. All that horse-riding and clean mountain air would be so wonderful for dear Paro.)

Meena didi said that the Amazon men had handed over their parcels at the door and departed.

I believed this.

Meena didi is not the sort to allow Amazon deliverymen to stroll into the house. Quite the opposite, in fact.

Conclusion: Not suspicious.

(Not even Darius suggested that the Amazon men were thieves in disguise.)

- The next visitor was Dr Prabhu. This was where things got interesting.

  Dr Prabhu had landed up at noon, acting as if he expected to meet four chicken-pox-riddled children. He'd ranted about how doctors deserved respect. He'd claimed that the mix-up was my fault, which had made it awkward for Meena didi to boot him out of the house.

  The doctor had insisted on parking on our moss green sofa and waiting for his next appointment. This meant that he'd spent about twenty minutes in the apartment. He'd asked Meena didi for water. Then he'd asked her for tea.

  Making tea had been difficult because the termite-killers had left the kitchen in a mess. Dr Prabhu had had more than enough time to slip in and out of my bedroom.

  Conclusion: Quite suspicious.

(Dr Prabhu had known that none of us would be at No. 492 Banyan Towers but had landed up anyhow. Did that mean he was a killer? Or did it just mean that he was a greedy doctor who wanted to get himself a cup of tea and bill us for an extra visit?)

- The next people to sit on the sofa had been Sir Renato, the dance teacher who couldn't dance, and Gurudev Mishr, the yoga teacher who looked like a bouncer at a seedy nightclub.

Gurudev Mishr had been determined to meet my father. He said he would meditate quietly on the brown rug till my father got home. It had taken thirty minutes and loads of ingenuity before Meena didi could get rid of him.

This was around the time that a couple of Amazon deliverymen and the ant and cockroach killers had landed up. Meena didi had been in and out of the living room and the unlovely duo had been left alone for short spells.

I had labelled the two men 'mildly suspicious'. I changed this to 'suspicious' after Sunidhi told us a little more about Gurudev Mishr.

Apparently, the regular yoga teacher had fallen ill in the middle of March. Gurudev Mishr had started teaching at The Orchard on April 1.

It was around then that Sandra Saldanha had fallen ill with malaria. She'd only returned to the yoga class for the last week of her life.

During her first class back, she had taken an uncharacteristic dislike to Gurudev Mishr. She'd watched him with disapproval during the hour-long session. Once the class was done, she had engaged him in a long conversation about 'drishti' and 'prana', after which she had decided that the new yoga teacher was a fraud.

Could Gurudev Mishr have panicked about losing his job? Even if he did, wasn't murder an extreme step? And what was Renato Sir's role in this?

Despite these loose ends, Gurudev Mishr made it to my list of suspects.

Conclusion:
Gurudev Mishr—Suspicious.
Sir Renato—Mildly suspicious.

- The next person to ring the doorbell had been Aarush Butalia, the rat-like brother of Aarti Butalia. He had come to borrow a Phillips screwdriver.

  Meena didi had gotten rid of him in five minutes. During this time, she had gone into the kitchen to do a cursory check for screwdrivers so there was a small chance that he could have nipped into my room and found the clue.

  Conclusion: Not suspicious unless we find a link with Sandra Saldanha.

(I could see Aarush Butalia as a killer of old women. It was just the job for him. So, I was disappointed that there was no other reason to suspect him.)

- The last of the Sunday procession was Aarti Butalia, who had landed up to help Meena didi find the Phillips screwdriver. She had bullied Meena didi into pulling out every single screwdriver, spanner and stapler-sort-of-object in the house.

Much to Meena didi's indignation, Aarti Butalia had drifted into my father's bedroom, wandered into the kitchen, helped herself to some Lonavala chikki, and opened drawers at random. It was possible that she had walked into my bedroom and opened my dressing table drawer. But why would she bother with a muddy scrap of paper?

Conclusion: Again, not suspicious unless we find a link with Sandra Saldanha.

(Nothing in the world would make me happier than to identify Aarti Butalia as the killer of Sandra Saldanha. But the others—who didn't know and dislike her the way I did—weren't interested in her as a suspect.

Still, to humour me, they agreed that we should find out if Aarti Butalia had a connection with Sandra Saldanha.)

'That's twelve men and one woman,' I said finally. 'But not one of them feels obviously right.'

'Maybe we're making a mistake by linking the missing chit to the killer,' Darius suggested.

'Or maybe we're missing the link,' Nihal mused. 'Somehow I feel if we look hard enough, we'll find it.'

Questions, Answers, More Questions

Monday, May 8

When in doubt, eat doughnuts. That seemed to be our motto on Monday morning.

Once more we headed to the dining table and the Krispy Kreme box. This time I chose a plain chocolate ring, which I held with my right hand so that I could take notes with my left. Ignoring Darius's remarks about lefties, I suggested that Nihal give us his update. 'Were you able to read the articles about the murder?' I asked. 'Did you find anything new?'

'I found one interesting detail,' Nihal said. 'The police say that Sandra Saldanha's phone is missing. I'm assuming that means the killer took it.'

'Dude, this is one cool killer,' Darius remarked almost admiringly. 'His perfect crime is messed up by someone standing outside and ringing the doorbell. But instead of panicking, he remembers to grab Sandra Saldanha's phone, finds a mask and even remembers to avoid the CCTV camera.'

Darius was right. There was a cold intelligence at work here that frightened me more than guns and knives and deadly poisons. Eager to change the topic, I asked Nihal if he had figured out how Sandra Saldanha's copy of *Poems of Strength and Courage* had landed up in the library.

'Sort of,' Nihal said, and began his story.

As soon as his mother got home from Bangalore on Sunday afternoon, Nihal had shown her *Poems of Strength and Courage*. 'My mother flipped,' Nihal laughed. 'She stared at the book and said that it had a black-red aura. Then she lit a lavender candle to get rid of the negative energy. Then she literally ran to the library with the book. She couldn't wait to get it out of the house.'

'What does a black-red aura mean?' Sunidhi asked just as I cried, 'What? We don't have the book any longer?'

'Sorry about that. My mother freaked that a murder victim's essence had entered the house,' Nihal said wryly. 'But I checked every single page thrice and I'm sure there was nothing else there.'

'Okay, we trust you,' Sunidhi said. 'But did the librarian tell your mom how the book had landed up in the library?'

'Yes,' Nihal said, before explaining that the librarian—whose name was Vasanthi Rao—had been unexpectedly helpful.

Vasanthi Rao had clearly been fond of Sandra Saldanha, and familiar with her habits. 'Miss Sandra borrowed books from four libraries,' she had said tearfully. 'She had four cane baskets in her living room—a brown basket for the books from the Mumbai University library, a green basket for the books from St Paul's library, a red basket for the books from Shemaroo. And a blue basket for the books from The Orchard library.'

Gajanan Shinde was sent to return books to the far-flung libraries. Kavita maushi—who cleaned for Sandra Saldanha and helped in the kitchen—was responsible for returning books to The Orchard library downstairs.

'Miss Sandra hadn't come down for almost a month because of malaria,' Vasanthi Rao told Nihal's mother. 'But she would send me the names of books over WhatsApp and Kavita maushi would come for them. The last time that Miss Sandra requested a book was Monday afternoon. She wanted a medical dictionary, which was a very unusual choice. I was going to ask her about it but then...the murder happened...'

Poems of Strength and Courage had landed up in the library on Friday morning—three days after the murder.

On Friday morning, the police had decided that Sandra Saldanha's apartment could be cleaned, and Kavita maushi had swept, swabbed, dusted, and emptied the fridge. She was on her way out when she spotted a pile of books in the blue basket. She carried them down to The Orchard library because that's what Sandra Saldanha would have wanted.

Vasanthi Rao was on leave that day, so Kavita maushi left the books on the librarian's table. A couple of hours later, Mrs Advani arrived and scooped them up for Nihal. Of the five books in the pile, *The Scarlet Pimpernel*, the medical dictionary, the book on yoga and the book on the Brontë sisters belonged to The Orchard library. The fifth book—*Poems of Strength and Courage*—had belonged to Sandra Saldanha.

'It's so strange,' Vasanthi Rao had said. 'Miss Sandra never ever mixed books up. That she should make such a mistake on her last day on earth...it feels wrong...'

The librarian's words poked at me because, like Sandra Saldanha, I never mess up with books. Was it really a coincidence that Sandra Saldanha had put the wrong book in the wrong basket? Or was it an act of desperation?

Could it be that Sandra Saldanha had opened the door to her killer, guessed that she was in trouble and dropped *Poems of Strength and Courage* into the blue basket? Hoping that somebody...maybe her friend Vasanthi Rao, maybe someone else...would open the book, find the paper, and begin to wonder?

When I returned to the present, Darius was talking about the CCTV cameras in Maple Towers. 'The camera on the 56th floor doesn't cover Sandra Saldanha's door,' he was saying. 'And there are at least three ways to enter and leave the apartment without being spotted. If you come outside, I can show you.'

A minute later, we were on the landing outside my apartment watching Darius demonstrate ways to avoid the CCTV camera. He was shuffling close to the wall when Sunidhi let out a bone-rattling yell. 'OMG, OMG. I should have thought of that. The person must have been checking the cameras. Of course.'

'What person?' we kept asking, but Sunidhi wouldn't say a word till we were back inside No. 492 with the door firmly shut.

'You remember, right, that I was supposed to talk to the security people in Maple Towers?' she asked finally. 'I waited till Tiwariji came on duty on Saturday evening because he's cleverer than Bhonsleji. Then I told him that I had a school assignment on CCTV cameras. First, we chatted about general stuff and then I got to the morning of the murder. I asked if Tiwariji had watched the CCTV footage again and if he'd spotted anything unusual.'

'Had he?' Darius asked with professional interest.

'No. But he mentioned that three days before she was killed, Sandra Saldanha had called the building security on the intercom. It was past midnight, and she was frantic. She said that there was somebody outside her apartment.'

'Poor Sandra Saldanha,' I exclaimed. 'Did the security guards spot anything?'

'Bhonsleji couldn't see anything on the CCTV. But Sandra Saldanha phoned again and said that somebody was pushing her door. She was almost crying so Tiwariji went upstairs but there was nobody there.'

'Did the guards do anything?' Darius asked.

'No,' Sunidhi said. 'They didn't take it seriously. They thought that Sandra Saldanha was shaky because she'd been so sick.'

We spent the next few minutes pondering over this and munching on nachos before Nihal remarked, 'Everyone keeps mentioning that Sandra Saldanha had been sick. It seems to have been a big thing.'

'It was,' Sunidhi said. 'She was stuck at home for three weeks. She'd only started leaving the house a few days before she was killed. And even then, she was only going for yoga. She didn't even have the energy to see her doctor.'

The moment we heard the word 'doctor', Nihal and I exchanged a glance.

'Was Dr Prabhu treating her?' we asked at the same moment.

Sunidhi didn't know, but she called her mother, who proved to be a storehouse of information about Sandra Saldanha's illness and recovery. Even better, she offered to come over the next morning to answer any other questions we might have.

'My mum's dying to see all of you,' Sunidhi giggled after hanging up. 'She keeps asking, "Is Paromita the girl with the shoulder-length hair? Is Darius the boy with the blue bicycle?" But wait, let me tell you what she said about Sandra Saldanha and Dr Prabhu.'

Sandra Saldanha had started treatment with her own doctor in Mahim. When the fever returned about ten days into the illness, she had called Dr Prabhu for an emergency visit. It was the first time she'd met the building doctor and he'd asked her to redo all her tests, questioned the malaria diagnosis and thrown up wild and terrifying possibilities.

When Sandra Saldanha's doctor—who was very senior and very stern—heard about this, he flipped. He called Dr Prabhu and gave him what Sunidhi's mother called 'a real tongue lashing'.

Dr Prabhu had reason to dislike Sandra Saldanha—and we had reason to open the HDFC diary and write a fourth name in the list of suspects.

Just as we had reason to stare when, less than five minutes later, Dr Prabhu huffed, puffed and whined his way into the dining room. He had a lot to say about how we had ignored his advice and wasted his time, but I heard very little. I was too busy wondering how to subtly slip Sandra Saldanha into the conversation.

I needn't have stressed. Darius was on the job.

'Dr Prabhu,' he said, with all the subtlety of a wrecking ball. 'We didn't know you had treated Sandra Saldanha just before she died.'

The wrecking ball hit Dr Prabhu in the stomach. He staggered and glared. Then he opened and closed his mouth a few times in the manner of a cartoon fish before barking, 'It's just talk.'

Darius smiled like a cartoon shark that has spotted its prey. 'But there's no smoke without fire, is there?' he asked in a silky voice.

The words had an unfortunate effect on the doctor. His face—a blobby, pale thing that looked like it had been made from grimy playdo—squished and flattened with indignation. His voice became more nasal, and his eyes acquired a pugnacious glint. 'You are children from good families,' he shrilled in a needle-thin voice. 'You should be attending to your studies, not listening to the gossip of low-class people.'

'But,' Darius said with an exaggerated smirk, 'sometimes the gossip is very interesting.'

Dr Prabhu galloped straight into Darius's trap. 'Every test or medicine I prescribe is for the good of the patient,' he screeched while fat drops of spit flew from his mouth. 'If I ask for one or two extra tests, if I recommend one or two extra medicines, if I say I will supply a nurse from a good bureau, it is for the good of the patient. How can a doctor treat his patients if they then turn around and accuse him of malpractice?'

Not realizing that he had just supplied us with a motive for murder, Dr Prabhu continued to rant. 'People have no work but to spoil the good name of others. That Sandra Saldanha was very sick when I visited her. Everything I did was out of concern. If she was still here, I would go to her and make her admit that she was wrong. I would MAKE her apologize.'

I had always viewed Dr Prabhu as a ridiculous figure. But in that moment, his clayey face distorted with rage, he looked capable of storming into Sandra Saldanha's house and demanding that she take back her words. He looked capable of murder.

What if Sandra Saldanha had refused to be bullied? Could that have led to her death?

'What are people saying about Dr Prabhu?' Sunidhi asked Darius after the doctor stormed out a few minutes later.

'No idea,' Darius laughed. 'If you push people enough, they usually dig their own graves. I thought that if I got Dr Prabhu mad enough, he would tell us himself.'

'He did,' I said grudgingly. Much as I hated to admit it, Darius and his obnoxiousness had their uses.

We were still discussing Dr Prabhu when Miss Rehana arrived. 'I have to leave soon,' she told us, looking both apologetic and excited. 'A detective has fallen ill in Prakash Sir's agency, so I've been asked to step in.'

'Oh wow,' Sunidhi exclaimed. 'What will you be doing?'

'Helping with the security for Gauri Kotecha's wedding,' Miss Rehana groaned. 'But I'm hoping it will lead to a proper job. This could be my big break. Now quickly tell me what you've been up to. I'll have to run when Mr Kotecha calls us for a meeting.'

Trying to be as brief as possible, we went over all that had happened since Saturday. Miss Rehana's eyes widened with each revelation. 'Wow,' she said finally. 'Fantastic detective work. But a pity about the missing paper. Prakash Sir wanted a clear copy to work on those codes. And he wanted an image of the other side of the paper as well. Paromita, did you make copies?'

'No,' I admitted.

Miss Rehana's face tightened and turned pink. 'That was not very clever of you. Prakash Sir will be mad at me. Just when I've started working for—' she was saying in a furious, un-Miss-Rehana-like voice when Nihal saved the day. He pulled out a small stack of papers from his bag and handed a sheet to each of us. 'Front and back,' he said. 'I always make copies.'

Clearly, Nihal and his invisibility had their uses too.

Miss Rehana had barely tucked the sheet in her bag when her phone rang. 'Sorry,' she said, jumping up. 'We'll talk tomorrow.'

'I had just one quick question—' I tried to say, but she was already out of the room.

Wishing that Miss Rehana wasn't always in a hurry, I flopped down on my bed. 'I really wanted to ask her what we should say to Sandra Saldanha's friends,' I sighed. 'I was hoping we could contact them today.'

'What friends?' Sunidhi asked. 'You haven't told us about them. Did you find anything interesting about Sandra Saldanha?'

'I found out quite a lot, actually,' I replied, before listing all that I now knew about the English teacher. Her love for plants; her book of poems; her nephew in Australia; her remarks about Mr Kotecha. And her three best friends—Zarine, Danielle and Vidya.

'I wanted to ask Miss Rehana what we should say to Zarine Bhavnagri when we call her,' I explained. 'But I guess we'll have to wait till tomorrow.'

'Perfect Paro messed up, Perfect Paro let the dogs out,' Darius began to chant, but zipped up when Sunidhi turned on him with unexpected ferocity.

'Shut up, Darius,' she snapped. 'Why don't you do something useful for a change. Call Miss Rehana so we can ask her about contacting the friends. I can't bear to wait till tomorrow. This is so exciting.'

Darius did as he was told but Miss Rehana's phone was switched off. After trying a couple of times, he posted a message on the Detective Club chat instead. 'We've found SS's frends. Wanted to call them. But what shud we say?'

After that there was nothing to do but to eat dhoklas and doughnuts and wrap up the day. The others were about to leave when I remembered something that had been troubling me. 'I keep feeling,' I said, 'that whoever stole the paper must have had a pretty good idea about where to look for it. Did you tell anyone where we put the paper?'

There was a shifty silence in the room before Darius spoke. 'Nobody knew that the paper was top secret,' he shrugged. 'I told Mr Khurana about it when I showed him the code. And my father and some guys on the Orchard football team.'

'You specifically told them where we'd put it?' I persisted.

'I might have,' Darius said so shadily that I guessed that the entire Orchard football team was sniggering about Paraparo and the brown ceramic cow.

'I definitely told some people,' Sunidhi confessed. 'I definitely told my mom and my dad and my sister. And my cousin in LA. And Tania from Gulmohar Towers. I don't know if I told all of them where we kept the paper, but I told some of them. I don't think any of them are suspects but they might have told others...'

'I didn't tell anyone,' Nihal said.

'And I may have told Adviti,' Sunidhi said, 'and I mentioned it to Nikki Aunty, who's Divisha's mother—'

Oh great. So all the cool girls were sniggering about Paraparo and the brown ceramic cow as well. We might as well have put up a neon sign on Marine Drive announcing that a mysterious scrap of paper belonging to the recently murdered Sandra Saldanha was in my dressing table drawer, waiting for anybody who was up to a spot of thievery.

Thanks so much, Sunidhi and Darius.

A Poem Shows the Way

Monday, May 8

Once the others left, I wandered around the house, wishing that I hadn't eaten the third doughnut (Apple Caramel, I think) and wondering what to do with myself.

I know that it sounds like I have no life outside the Detective Club, but that's not true. Under normal circumstances, I'm fully busy with school and homework and my coding class and my schoolfriends. But for the moment, school is closed, Samhita and Myra are travelling, and I'm stuck at home with chicken pox. So there's really not much to do other than drink green tea and read books.

After junking on my phone for a bit, I decided that it was time for Book No. 18.

I was trying to choose between *To All the Boys I've Loved Before* and *The Sisterhood of the Travelling Pants* when, on a whim, I chose a third book altogether. Then promptly regretted my decision.

The View from a High Window had been published all the way back in 2007. What could it possibly tell me about the murder of its author?

Still, now that I had bought Sandra Saldanha's collection of poems, I felt compelled to read it. I'm not a poetry person, so it was lucky that the book was just 130 pages long. I decided to skim through the poems at the rate of one per minute and was well on track till I reached Page 43. And froze.

Right on top of the page were the words 'Moody and D'. You can hardly blame me for dropping my Kindle.

Moody.

The word had been written in thick marker at the top of the mud-stained scrap of paper that Nihal had found tucked between the pages of Sandra Saldanha's book.

On my Kindle too, the word leapt out in large, bold letters.

This felt like more than a coincidence.

Sandra Saldanha wrote poetry in a variety of styles. Some of her poems rhymed and made instant sense. Others, though, were written in scattered, fragmented lines that looked like a game of Scrabble. Unfortunately, 'Moody and D' belonged to the Scrabble category. I had to read it many, many times before things clicked in my head.

If you think I'm exaggerating, see for yourself:

Moody and D

Bye bye
TWO
B
O
Y
S
Spotted last at Chetan Tea Stall

vada pav, Gold Spot
rusted gate, puddled path
drowsing outside Kasara Station

more is twisted than just the gate

memories bleached like clothes in the noonday sun
blackbird singing in the dead of night

Moody
o
o
o
oozing
oozing squeezing

Oozing blood
Oozing death

Not all that is to be handled with care is fragile
Not all that is seen is to be believed

Moody and D

What? What did this even mean? With every reading, my headache and confusion grew. At least till I focused on Kasara Station.

Kasara is one of those far-away towns that you drive past on your way to somewhere else. Just a name on a dusty highway. So why did it suddenly feel familiar and important? As if I'd encountered it in the last day or two?

I'd gone through so many poems, articles, interviews, columns over the last few days that the filing system in my head had collapsed. Fortunately, the HDFC diary was more reliable. I read through my notes till I found what I was looking for. All the way back in 1999, Sandra Saldanha had written an article about two students from St Paul's College who had vanished while trekking in the Western Ghats.

The boys had started their trek from Kasara.

Bye bye...
two boys...
Spotted last at Chetan Tea Stall

Could Moody and D be the two missing boys?

No matter how hard I hunted, neither the poem nor Google provided an answer. (Sandra Saldanha hadn't mentioned the names of the boys in her article, and googling Moody and D doesn't get you very far.)

Still, I posted a picture of the poem on the Detective Club chat and wrote: Moody and D could be students of SS who vanished while trekking in 1997

Darius Engineer replied, saying that 'Moody and D' was the worst poem he'd read in his life and that it helped him to value the *Poems of Strength and Courage*. I had just sent two laughing emojis when a message from Miss Rehana flashed on the chat:

Just heard that the police have released driver
Gajanan Shinde

Most interested to hear about SS's friends

Where did you find this poem?

Don't do anything re friends till we have a proper talk.
Important to do this properly

See you tomorrow

A Useful Meeting

Tuesday, May 9

Sunidhi's mother was a rounder, dimplier version of Sunidhi. She bounced into the apartment with a box of vanilla cupcakes, greeted each one of us by name, sat on the moss green sofa and regretfully turned down my offer of mango ice cream.

'Avoiding sweets,' she explained. 'But you young detectives must eat. You need all the energy. Now tell me what you want to know about Sandra. We were both among the first to move into Maple Towers in 2014. We did yoga together for almost six years. I think Sandra and I got to know each other quite well.'

We'd spent the morning writing down a list of important questions, but Nihal began by asking one that we hadn't discussed.

'Did you like Sandra Saldanha?' he asked.

Sunidhi's mother didn't hesitate. 'Very much,' she said. 'There was something essentially good about her. You always knew she would do the right thing.'

Glancing at the trusty HDFC diary, I asked the next question. 'Do you remember how Sandra Saldanha was during the last week of April? Did she seem scared or worried?'

Mrs Menon took her time answering. 'Sandra had been unwell,' she said finally. 'She missed almost three weeks of yoga. In fact, I don't think she left the house at all during those three weeks. And then she attended only two classes before...before she died.'

'On which days are your yoga classes?' Darius asked.

'Tuesdays and Fridays, evening batch,' Sunidhi's mother said. 'The first yoga class that Sandra attended after her illness was on a Tuesday. During that class she became quite agitated about the new yoga teacher—Gurudev Mishr—because she thought he was a fake.'

'Sunidhi told us about that,' I said. 'Do you also feel he's a fraud?'

Again, Mrs Menon paused before saying, 'I don't know if he's a fraud, but he doesn't have the right vibe for a yoga teacher. And he got quite aggressive with Sandra when she had a chat with him.'

Sunidhi, who had been bobbing vigorously while her mother spoke, could no longer contain herself. 'Tell them what happened during the next class,' she burst out. 'The one on Friday. That's too interesting.'

Nodding, her mother said, 'The Friday class itself was uneventful. Sandra seemed tired and didn't say anything more about the yoga teacher. But it was after class that she dropped the oregano that she had potted for Rati Ginwala.'

'Dropped the oregano?' I repeated blankly.

'Yes. It was very odd,' Mrs Menon said. 'The yoga class happens in a room next to the gym. After class, four of us left together. We'd just stepped onto the road near the West Lawn when Sandra let out a sound. I couldn't tell if she'd coughed or screamed. She stopped walking and stared straight ahead. I noticed that she'd turned completely white, and her hands were shaking so much that she dropped the pot. We thought she was going to faint. I wanted her to sit down and drink water, but she insisted on going straight home. I assumed that it happened because of her illness...but now I wonder...'

'Wonder what?' we chorused.

'Wonder if she saw someone...or something...that really frightened her...something bad...'

As Mrs Menon spoke, I recalled Sunday evening and my conviction that evil was skulking just outside the door. Once again, I could feel fear—like a hairy spider—crawl down my spine.

'Was there anything happening on the West Lawn?' Nihal asked after an uneasy pause.

'I can't be sure, but I think it was the usual,' Mrs Menon said. 'People walking dogs. Mr Kotecha was around because I noticed his car and some security people...there were a bunch of children in the Pavilion, and I remember looking out for Sunidhi...and I think some workmen were decorating the stage and checking wires for Gauri Kotecha's sangeet...I think...'

'The sangeet was two days later, on Sunday,' Sunidhi confirmed. 'Remember? Nobody could sleep because it was so loud. But tell them what happened next.'

'Sandra and I walked to Maple Towers together,' Mrs Menon said slowly. 'I insisted on dropping her to her door. When she stepped into her apartment, Sandra said something I didn't properly catch. Something odd...'

'What?'

'It sounded like...not a ghost after all...'

'Not a ghost after all?' we echoed.

'Something like that, but I could be wrong. At that point I had no idea that it could be important.'

'What happened next?' Darius asked.

'Nothing,' Sunidhi's mother said sadly. 'As I was leaving, I heard Sandra locking and bolting her door. I wondered why, but I didn't ask. It was the last time that I saw her. She was dead before the next yoga class on Tuesday...'

'Today is Tuesday,' Nihal remarked in a shaky voice. 'It's been exactly one week.'

Noticing our stricken expressions, Sunidhi's mother tried to change the subject. She was chatting about summer plans and suggesting we go over for dinner, when Darius cut in abruptly. 'Everybody keeps saying that Sandra Saldanha was kind and sweet and generous,' he said. 'But she must have done *something* to get herself murdered.'

'That's rubbish,' both Sunidhi and I started to say, but Mrs Menon looked thoughtful.

'I don't think it was something she did,' she said finally. 'But it could have been something she was. Sandra was kind and generous, but she was also determined and stubborn. For example, she must have written at least ten emails to Mr Kotecha and to the Orchard Building Society objecting to the way that the West Lawn had been taken over by Gauri Kotecha's wedding.'

'Was Mr Kotecha bothered?' Nihal asked.

'Probably not,' Mrs Menon replied. 'But what I'm trying to say is that if Sandra felt something was wrong, she couldn't ignore it. Maybe that's what got her into trouble.'

An Even More Useful Meeting

Tuesday, May 9

After Sunidhi's mother left, we were restless. Darius fiddled with the brown contents of his tub of Poo Dough. (I'm not lying. It is a thing.) Sunidhi practised her butterfly leaps and hurt her foot badly. Even the usually still Nihal fidgeted with his blue backpack.

'Let's just contact Zarine Bhavnagri,' Sunidhi said for the millionth time. 'I really can't understand what the problem is.'

The problem was Miss Rehana.

Miss Rehana didn't trust us to talk to Sandra Saldanha's friends by ourselves. Her fury of yesterday had given us a sneak peek into what would happen if we disobeyed her. 'It's best to wait,' I said. 'It's just a few hours. I don't want to make her mad again.'

'Miss Rehana was scary yesterday,' Sunidhi agreed. 'I think she really wants the job with Prakash Talwar's agency. She's afraid that we will mess things up and that Prakash Talwar will think she's a bad detective. But I still don't see why we just can't contact—'

'It's really not a good idea,' I said for what felt like the thousandth time. 'But what do the rest of you feel?'

For once, Darius was on my side. 'Even if we call Zarine Bhavnagri, what will we say?' he asked. 'That we are a bunch of kids and that we found a clue connected with the death of Sandra Saldanha but instead of handing it to the police, we decided to play detective?'

'Zarine Bhavnagri will hang up in ten seconds,' Nihal agreed.

It was at this point that Sunidhi played her ace. 'I don't think we should phone,' she said. 'I think we should just land up. It's much more difficult to be rude in person than on the phone. Zarine Bhavnagri's studio is just ten minutes by car. And it's right next to that frozen yoghurt place. Last time I had the raspberry flavour with the marshmallow fluff topping and white chocolate sprinklies. It was divine.'

There are few things in the world that can change minds as quickly as frozen raspberry yoghurt topped with marshmallow fluff and white chocolate sprinklies. Being the gormless creatures that they were, Darius and Nihal promptly changed their minds.

'Come on, Perfect Paro,' Darius urged. 'Stop being a teacher's pet. I can book an Uber to take us.'

'The whole trip will take less than an hour,' Nihal agreed.

Hello? Didn't anybody else remember that we had chicken pox? That we were not supposed to be wandering around Mumbai, shedding our scabs?

'No,' I said primly.

'Why?'

'For many reasons,' I replied. 'Firstly, because we are contagious. Secondly, I'm not allowed to leave The Orchard without permission. Thirdly, I'm not allowed to use an Uber without an adult.'

'I've looked up a bunch of medical websites,' Nihal said. 'They all agree that we don't need to quarantine after Day Five.'

'And if you add Nihal's, Sunidhi's and my ages, it's equal to an adult,' Darius added. 'Maybe even two adults.'

'Please Paromita, please, please,' Sunidhi jumped in. 'Aren't you dying to meet Sandra Saldanha's best friend and ask her everything? Please let's go. Please agree.'

I agreed eventually. Peer pressure is a terrible thing.

Five minutes later, Darius booked the Uber and we sneaked out of Banyan Towers.

There were two bad moments before we got to the Uber. As we stepped out of the building into the blazing summer-holiday sunshine, Sunidhi noticed a thin woman in pink leotards about ten steps ahead of us and mumbled, 'Oh no. Miss Heena. She's just the sort to make a big deal if she sees four chicken poxy kids roaming around. Let's cut through the lawn.'

The second bad moment came when we spotted Dr Prabhu, straight and alert in the Pavilion. He was standing between two men—one, tall and imposing; the other, short and shrunken. The little group was being addressed by Mr Kotecha, who was blaring at the top of his lungs, 'Prakashji, I have full faith in you. You are the big boss for the evening. Dr Prabhu, Sudeshji and even I will all take instructions from you. Nothing must go wrong with even one of the two thousand guests.'

The tall man smiled and nodded, and I realized that I had just caught my first glimpse of Prakash Talwar. He looked exactly like a famous detective should. Strong, commanding, with a Sherlock Holmes nose.

I tried to linger and eavesdrop, but Darius gave me a poke in the ribs. 'Hurry,' he hissed. 'Prabhu might spot us, and the Uber has arrived.'

The Uber was waiting outside The Orchard gate. Traffic was light and eight minutes later we were inside one of those old mill compounds, which are now full of shops and restaurants with names like The Silk Thread Company and The Duck and the Dram.

The Uber dropped us outside a small, two-storey structure painted the happy pink of cotton candy. The ground floor was occupied by a store selling plush sofas of the kind that Aarti Butalia would promptly have draped herself upon.

The first floor housed Studio Zafa. And—with some luck—Zarine Bhavnagri.

Glancing uncertainly at each other, we climbed the narrow staircase to a door painted over with purple swirls. After staring at it nervously for a moment, Sunidhi pushed it open and peeped into a tiny, bright, white room with a single table, a single chair and a youngish woman wearing a steel-grey dress and a steel-grey expression.

The woman's expression became even greyer when she realized that we were about to invade her immaculate office. Jumping to her feet, she took three steps and blocked the door. 'Can I help you?' she demanded in the most unhelpful manner imaginable.

We explained that we wanted to meet Zarine Bhavnagri.

'Do you have an appointment?' the woman barked. We admitted that we didn't.

'Are you here to see the Aasman Collection?' she asked. We admitted that we weren't.

'If you tell me your business, I will ask madam,' she said. We mumbled that we could only tell madam our business.

This didn't go down well. The steely creature was instructing us to send an email—to which she would respond within a fortnight—when a deep, laughing voice emerged from inside the studio. 'Now Shraddha, who are you terrorizing this time?'

'Some *children* have come to meet you,' Shraddha announced in the same tone that she would have used to announce a pack of naked mole rats.

'Children?' the big voice clarified.

'Yes. And they are not even here to see the Aasman Collection.'

'I should hope not,' the voice laughed. 'The Aasman Collection is not at all appropriate for children. But let them come in and let's find out what they want. It's not often that we get children at our doorstep.'

Shraddha pursed her lips but stepped aside so that we could squeeze into the little white room. This was a challenge because at least half the space was occupied by the owner of the big voice—a substantial woman wearing a grey astronaut outfit and goggles strapped onto her head with a neon green band.

'We're so sorry to disturb you but we wanted to meet Zarine Bhavnagri,' Sunidhi managed to say, while the rest of us gawped.

'This is she,' the woman replied. 'Or this is her. I would need Sandra to tell me—'

She broke off abruptly, but the mention of Sandra Saldanha prodded us out of our stupor.

We introduced ourselves to Zarine Bhavnagri in a confusing chorus. Then Sunidhi explained that we all lived in The Orchard by Kotecha. 'We wanted to talk to you about something important connected with Sandra Saldanha,' she said. 'It will only take a few minutes.'

Shraddha raised a hand and tutted. 'No,' she exclaimed to Zarine Bhavnagri. 'I don't think—'

We couldn't see Zarine's eyes behind the dark, round glasses, but her posture was wary. 'I'm not sure it's a good idea—'

Before Zarine could complete her sentence, however, Sunidhi hurried on. 'We found a scrap of paper on which Sandra Saldanha had written some stuff,' she said urgently. 'And we think it could be linked to her death. We just want to talk to you for ten minutes.'

'Some stuff about balloons bursting and Christina Rossetti,' I added, trying to talk over the objection-spouting Shraddha. 'And Moody—'

'Moody?' Zarine Bhavnagri frowned. 'Did you say Moody?'

After that, things moved quickly. Zarine Bhavnagri pulled off her goggles, pointed us into a large room with sky-blue walls and twisty metal creations and had Shraddha fetch four bottles of Limca. 'Sit,' she ordered. 'Drink. Tell me.'

We did as we were told. We sat on a long black sofa, sipped Limca and spoke. We told her about the scrap of paper with the peculiar scribbles, and about the strange way in which it had gone missing. It was at this point that Zarine held up her hand and said, 'Wait. I need to talk to the others.'

Then she went into the little white room and made two calls. One was brief. The other involved a long, hushed conversation. 'Five o'clock this evening,' she announced when she returned to the room. 'Come to The Gymkhana. We will all be there.'

As we walked out of Studio Zafa, I had a familiar sensation in my stomach. The feeling you get when you reach the top of a tall slide and know that one way or another, you will soon be hurtling towards the bottom.

Good News and a Warning

Tuesday, May 9

Miss Rehana was bright-eyed and excited when she arrived at 2.45 p.m.

'Prakash Sir is investigating the Saldanha murder,' she announced as soon as she walked into my bedroom. 'Mr Kotecha has asked him to give the case top priority. Isn't that great? It's in the best possible hands.'

The news caused an uproar. Why would Mr Kotecha—who had never been a sensitive, neighbour-loving sort—spend big bucks on solving the murder of a virtual stranger? Was he worried that there was a psychopath at large? Or that The Orchard would get a bad reputation? Or that the sale of apartments in The Arboretum by Kotecha would be hit by the murder?

We swapped theories till Miss Rehana announced that she had another surprise for us. 'Prakash Sir is very impressed by your powers of observation and reasoning,' she smiled. 'He's been following your progress with interest. He's happy to have a chat with you if you need his advice.'

The idea of being mentored by Mumbai's most famous detective caused another uproar.

'Can we meet him?' I asked.

'Sir has been unwell,' Miss Rehana said. 'And he's madly busy with the Gauri Kotecha wedding. But maybe he can do a short call tomorrow so that you can ask him about Sandra Saldanha's friends. I think it will be best if he talks to them—'

'Miss Rehana, you won't believe it,' Sunidhi interrupted happily. 'We've already gone and met Zarine Bhavnagri and—'

I nudged Sunidhi, but it was too late. Miss Rehana looked up sharply. 'What?' she barked. 'You went and met who?'

'Zarine Bhavnagri was one of Sandra Saldanha's best friends,' Sunidhi replied. 'Her studio is just ten minutes from—'

With every word that Sunidhi uttered, Miss Rehana looked more tight-lipped and white-faced. 'Did you tell anyone that you were going?' she demanded as soon as Sunidhi was done. 'Did you take along an adult? How did you even get there?'

'Uber,' Sunidhi replied.

'Uber? Alone? Without an adult? Are all of you crazy?' Miss Rehana choked, before launching into a rant. She told us that we had behaved in a foolish manner. That this was a murder investigation, which meant that there was a murderer out there. To go to an old mill compound to meet a stranger without checking with our parents was reckless and dangerous. Prakash Sir would be livid if we had muddied the waters or alerted witnesses by conducting clumsy interviews. And why, why, why, hadn't we just called her?

'We tried to call you yesterday, but your phone was switched off,' Nihal replied. 'And I don't think we messed anything up. So far nobody has even contacted Sandra Saldanha's friends. At least Paromita found them.'

Miss Rehana heard the rare indignation in his voice and made an effort to calm down. She admitted that it was very clever of us to have found Sandra Saldanha's friends. Then she explained that her personal phone was often switched off because Prakash Talwar expected his detectives to use agency phones while working. 'I'll add that number to the chat,' she said. 'But before I forget, did Sandra Saldanha's friend have anything interesting to say?'

'Not really,' Darius lied smoothly. 'Zarine Bhavnagri said she would call if she remembered anything.'

'Okay. Let me know if she gets in touch. And please, please promise me that you won't go meeting more strangers. I'm adding the second phone number to the chat so if anything—ANYTHING—comes up, please check with me.'

'Yes, Miss Rehana,' we agreed with solemn faces and cheating hearts.

Miss Rehana was a good enough detective to guess that something was afoot—but she had no way of knowing that in less than two hours we would be doing exactly what she had warned us against. That at 5 p.m. that evening, we were meeting Zarine, Danielle and Vidya at The Gymkhana.

We were saved from further interrogation by a phone call. Miss Rehana took the call, jumped to her feet and hurried to the door saying, 'Thank god, this Gauri Kotecha wedding wraps up tomorrow. Two Bollywood stars are performing, and three ministers are attending, so the security is unreal. Mr Kotecha has had six meetings with Prakash Sir over the last two days.'

'Which Bollywood stars?' Sunidhi asked.

'It's a secret for the moment,' Miss Rehana laughed. 'But I bet every security guard, driver and dhobi knows. Just ask one of them.'

'Will you be at the wedding?' Darius asked.

'The entire team of Talwar Kumar Investigations will be there in fancy clothes, pretending to be wedding guests,' Miss Rehana groaned as she opened the door and waved to us. 'Now all of you please, please remember that this is a murder investigation. Somebody out there has killed once and could kill again. And please remember that this person could even be someone you know and trust.'

Miss Rehana's warning sat in the room long after she left. 'Maybe we shouldn't go this evening,' I half whispered. 'It's true that the killer could be almost anyone.'

'But not Zarine, Danielle or Vidya,' Sunidhi exclaimed. 'We're hardly risking danger by meeting three white-haired grannies who will give us cake and nimbu pani.'

'And if we don't go, we may never get answers,' Nihal pointed out. 'That would be worse.'

Nihal was right. The possibility of never knowing was worse than the possibility of encountering a killer. This was an appointment we had to keep.

An Evening at the Gymkhana

Tuesday, May 9

Let me say this upfront. There was nothing cuddly and grandmotherly about Zarine, Danielle or Vidya. They stared at us with examiners' eyes as we walked down the long veranda of The Gymkhana. They didn't smile when we introduced ourselves. They didn't ply us with cake or nimbu pani.

The Gymkhana is one of those posh clubs with heavy white napkins, billiards rooms, card rooms and rules about children, mobile phones, footwear, T-shirts and sleeves. Zarine, Danielle and Vidya were at the far end of the veranda, sitting on cane armchairs around a low, glass-topped table loaded with silver teapots, white cups and plates of chutney sandwiches. They gestured towards a cane three-seater, and we perched on it in an intimidated row.

Zarine had replaced her astronaut suit with jeans and a short blue kurta. Somehow, these everyday clothes made her appear even more eccentric. She was obviously a bit of a celebrity, and people kept stopping to coo, 'How was the show in Brussels?'

Two feet away, Danielle was half-reclining on her armchair and watching the world with narrowed eyes and a wry smile. She had grey, shoulder-length hair, a husky voice, and a hacking cough. Her saree was very purple, her blouse was cut very low, and her bra straps were very visible. She didn't at all fit my image of a college professor.

Vidya, on the other hand, looked exactly as a college professor should. She was wearing a neat kurta, neat spectacles and a neat bun. She sat very straight and scrutinized us, almost as if she was grading us, while we stammered out our explanation. I got the feeling that she was suspicious of us—and her first sentence proved this. 'I'm wondering,' she said, 'why you didn't hand over the book and the paper to the police. Wouldn't that have been the right and sensible thing to do?'

This was the question we'd been dreading. We could hardly admit that we'd jumped into the investigation for—to borrow a phrase from Meena didi—time pass. And that by the time we realized it wasn't a game, we were in it too deep. 'We...we...' I started to say when we got help from an unexpected source.

'I disagree,' Danielle rasped. 'I would trust a starving maneater more than I would trust the police. The police are tools of the system, only interested in maintaining status quo and pinning the crime on some helpless driver or labourer.'

'But they are better equipped to investigate a crime than little children,' Vidya remonstrated.

'These children are not all that little. The fact that they tracked us down proves that they are quite capable. The police haven't even bothered to talk to us.'

'Danielle, they are thirteen- and fourteen-year-olds. Just a few years older than my grandchildren. I don't feel comfortable about this,' Vidya snapped, pursed her lips, and leaned back in her armchair, as if opting out of the conversation. 'You seem to forget that this is a murder.'

'How can I forget that this is murder?' Danielle spluttered and coughed at Vidya, before turning to us and examining us with sharp eyes. 'Explain in one line what you want from us.'

Feeling more than ever like we were in the middle of a critical exam, the four of us glanced at each other before Sunidhi mumbled, 'We were wondering, did you meet Sandra Saldanha on the Saturday before...it happened?'

'Yes,' Zarine boomed. 'We did. We spent three hours together at this very table.'

'Did she behave different in any way?' I pounced. 'Did she seem upset or scared?'

'We were meeting after a whole month because Sandra had been ill, and Zarine had been travelling,'

Danielle said as she sucked on her cigarette. 'I got the feeling that Sandra was preoccupied. That there was something troubling her.'

'I noticed that too,' Zarine said. 'I thought it was because she was still weak. And because she was so angry with that horrible man. Kutti, Kachoo, Kutroo...'

'Kotecha,' Danielle supplied. 'The builder.'

Next to me, I could feel Nihal stiffen. Mr Kotecha was the first name on our list of suspects. Had we been right all along?

'Why was she angry with Mr Kotecha?' Darius asked.

'It was that bloody wedding,' Danielle exploded.

She sounded so distressed that Vidya leaned forward to pat her friend's arm and reluctantly took over the story. 'I am talking to you children against my better judgement,' she sighed. 'Do your parents even know that you are here and getting involved in this ugliness?'

There was no option but to lie. We muttered unconvincing things like 'they know' and 'they don't mind' and 'they are fine with it'. Vidya raised an eyebrow and shook her head, but she decided to believe us.

'Sandra struggled with insomnia. And the Kotecha wedding didn't help matters. There was one miserable night...Wednesday? Thursday? When she finally fell asleep around 2 a.m. only to be woken by loud drums, guitars, that sort of thing. They were doing a soundcheck for some band that was to perform the next day.'

'Wednesday night,' Sunidhi confirmed. 'I had my last exam the next day—Geography. My father went down to complain but the security people stopped him and acted like he was trying to bomb the place or something.'

'Sandra went downstairs too but everyone ignored her,' Vidya said in her flat voice. 'She called to tell me about it the next day. She said she was so tired that she was seeing ghosts.'

Seeing ghosts?

The four of us sat up so suddenly that the cane seat moaned in protest. On Thursday morning, Sandra Saldanha had told Vidya that she was seeing ghosts. The very next day, on Friday, she had said something to Sunidhi's mother about it not being a ghost after all. What could it mean?

'Did Sandra Saldanha talk about seeing ghosts on that last Saturday when you met?' Darius asked eagerly. 'Did she say anything unusual? Did she talk about Mr Kotecha? Or about anybody else?'

The three women sitting across from us glanced at each other. We could almost hear the question zipping between them. Should we trust these children?

Zarine, the stocky sculptor, looked uncertain.

Vidya, the neat biology teacher, looked reluctant.

Danielle, the free-spirited English teacher, looked reckless and angry. 'There was one subject that Sandra kept returning to on that Saturday,' she said roughly.

'Moody and Dheeraj. You mentioned Moody when you went to meet Zarine. Why don't you start by telling us what you know about him?'

A challenge had been issued—and it was clear that everything depended on our response. Feeling sick with nerves, I cleared my throat and said, 'We are not sure, but we think that Moody was one of two boys who went for a trek during the monsoons in 1997 and vanished.'

For a few seconds nobody spoke. Then Danielle began to laugh. 'Full marks,' she exclaimed before turning to her friends and asking, 'Do you really think the police would have gotten this far? These children deserve answers.'

Zarine smiled and even Vidya unbent enough to say, 'They do seem to know a lot.'

Two minutes later—after Zarine had hailed the hovering waiter and ordered a round of Limcas for us—Danielle began her account. 'Vidya, Sandra and I started teaching at St Paul's College at around the same time,' she said. 'Sandra was an extraordinarily committed teacher and ran a Thursday Study Group for students who were struggling. She provided them with a quiet space to work, helped them to plan timetables, that sort of thing. Moody and Dheeraj were regulars at the Study Group. Dheeraj was academically weak. And Moody needed a quiet space to study.'

Danielle paused to pour herself pale tea from the teapot before continuing. 'Dheeraj was a History student.

He was a bulky, lumbering boy with the handwriting of a kindergartener. I remember wondering how he had managed to get admission into college even. He was dull but devoted to Sandra. I think he was from an immensely wealthy family, but he was having problems with his parents. Sandra insisted that Dheeraj had a good heart. But then Sandra insisted that most people had good hearts. She was a fool.'

Grabbing her handbag, Danielle pulled out a handkerchief and wiped her eyes. 'I knew Moody because he was an English student. Charming boy. There was something vulnerable about him. I can't remember if he limped, but he was small-built and fragile. I think his parents were dead and he lived with some truly unpleasant cousins. The cousins wanted Moody out of the house. Sandra was so upset about this that she actually went and met the cousins.'

'Didn't Moody have a health issue?' Zarine interrupted. 'One of those illnesses involving bleeding? I remember Sandra had to drive him to hospital once.'

'Moody had haemophilia,' Vidya nodded. 'It's a disorder in which the blood doesn't clot properly. Even a small injury—or something like the loss of a tooth—can cause heavy bleeding. I think his was quite severe.'

Listening to Vidya's words, I felt a moment of confused recognition—the feeling you get when you see a man walking past and know that you've met him before but can't remember where. What had Vidya said that I'd encountered before?

I puzzled over this while the waiter brought the Limcas. He was arranging them in a straight line on the glass table when two words popped into my head. 'Oozing blood,' I blurted out and turned red when seven pairs of eyes swivelled to stare at me.

The waiter was the most fascinated—and Zarine the most alarmed.

'Are you hurt?' she asked nervously.

'That's a line from a poem by Sandra Saldanha,' I replied, pulling out my phone, finding the picture of 'Moody and D' and handing it to Danielle. 'It just popped into my head.'

Danielle read the poem with a faraway look in her eyes. 'Moody oozed blood on more than one occasion,' she said eventually, as she passed my phone to Zarine.

While Vidya and Zarine read the poem, the rest of us sipped our drinks and thought about missing boys, bodies smashing into swimming pools and blood that wouldn't stop flowing. Through it all, I had the niggling feeling that there was another connection. Another face in a passing bus that I should have recognized.

'Why did Moody and Dheeraj go for the trek together?' Nihal asked after Zarine handed my phone back to me. 'And what exactly happened to them?'

'Trekking during the monsoons was a favourite activity at St Paul's,' Danielle said. 'I think a biggish group was supposed to go but the others dropped out. These two decided to carry on.'

'Were Moody and D special friends?' Sunidhi asked.

'They were part of a group of five or six students,' Danielle shrugged. 'I don't remember any of them too well. But Vidya might.'

'I remember the two girls,' Vidya said. 'Ami was quite brilliant and eventually became a marine biologist. The other one was Rina or Radha or something. That pretty dancer. I think she was Moody's girlfriend, but I could be wrong.'

'Yes, yes,' Danielle exclaimed. 'I remember now. The girls opted out of the trek because it was pouring. That Rina girl never forgave herself. Dropped out of college and had a breakdown. In a way she disappeared as well. So many lives destroyed.'

For a moment, I imagined how Moody's and Dheeraj's friends must have felt as they waited for news. The anxiety gradually replaced by hopelessness and guilt.

'But how could the boys have disappeared so completely,' I asked. 'Didn't the police look for them?'

'All we know is that Moody and Dheeraj took a train, alighted at Kasara, walked out of the station and vanished,' Vidya said. 'Dheeraj's parents had gone on a pilgrimage. Moody's cousins had assumed that he was sleeping at a friend's house. Dheeraj's parents contacted the police when they got back, but by then there was no trace of the boys. Initially, we assumed that it was a hiking accident.'

'It wasn't?' I asked, although I think I already knew.

'It's confusing,' Vidya said. 'It turned out that the bank accounts belonging to the two boys, as well as a joint account belonging to Dheeraj's father had been emptied out. Also, a couple of months after they disappeared, Dheeraj's parents received a note from him.'

'What did it say?' Nihal asked.

'The note said something like "You were always ashamed of me. Now you won't have to see me any longer." The letter had been posted from some other city. Ahmedabad? Surat? Something like that. After that, the police wondered if the two boys had run away from home. Both, in their own ways, were rolling stones.'

'Then?'

'There were no fresh developments for a long time,' Danielle said. 'And then, ten years later they found the remains.'

'The remains?' Sunidhi and Darius gasped loud enough for the people at the next table to look up. 'Whose remains?'

'Danielle, stop exaggerating and scaring the children,' Vidya frowned. 'I think it was in 2008 or 2009. A trekker fell into a ditch in the jungles near Kasara and found a wallet. The wallet had Moody's college identity card. When the police searched the area, they found denim fragments with traces of blood.'

'Then?' we chorused.

'It seemed evident that unlike Dheeraj, Moody hadn't emerged alive from that jungle. So the police assumed that Dheeraj had killed Moody. Or, at least, left him to bleed away on the hillside, and profited from his death by emptying his bank account.'

Despite the hot, soupy summer evening, I shivered. A series of images flashed before me: Two boys walking into the wet jungle. A boy bleeding unstoppably on a lonely hillside. A wallet lying in a ditch, waiting to be discovered.

'Of course, Sandra absolutely refused to believe it,' Danielle continued after a long bout of coughing. 'She insisted that it must have been an accident. That Dheeraj was not a killer. That the police were slapdash and incompetent. That they should conduct a full investigation, DNA testing, that sort of thing. But no one else found the idea so incredible.'

A tired silence descended on our table. Vidya brushed non-existent crumbs off her white kurta and checked the time on her silver watch. Danielle slumped in her chair, looking as crumpled as her purple saree. Zarine indicated to the waiter that he should fetch the bill. The evening was wrapping up, but there was still so much we didn't know.

'Not all that is to be handled with care is fragile / Not all that is to be seen is to be believed,' I said softly.

Only Danielle caught the reference—she had been an English teacher, after all. 'I've been wondering about the poem too,' she said. 'Very cryptic.'

Darius, though, ignored our conversation and returned to the central question: 'What exactly did Sandra Saldanha say about Moody and Dheeraj on Saturday?'

'Sandra was trying to remember Moody's real name,' Zarine replied.

'She didn't know Moody's real name?' Sunidhi squawked. 'I thought she knew him very well.'

Danielle laughed. 'Oh, the unforgiving nature of youth,' she cried. 'Sandra did know Moody well, and at that point she must have known his real name. But everybody only ever called him Moody. And the thing about growing old is that things blur and smudge...'

'Why Moody?' Nihal asked. 'Was he moody?'

'Moody was short for something,' Zarine said. 'Something like Michael D'Souza.'

'Or Martin D'Costa,' Danielle added. 'Something along those lines.'

We stopped speaking while the waiter cleared the teacups, Limca bottles and plates. The tables in the long veranda were filling up fast. Groups of teenagers settling down for a snack and a giggle. Middle-aged men chatting over nimbu pani after a game of tennis.

Looking around, I was astonished to see that the sun had dipped behind a mango tree and that dusk had crept in. It was time to head back to The Orchard. Right on cue, Vidya announced that she needed to leave. 'I'm in charge of the grandchildren tonight,' she said. 'And it's getting late.'

'We only have one question left,' Darius said urgently. 'What was the burst balloon and the book without words and Rossetti?'

'Oh yes,' Danielle said. 'Those crumbling memento mori.'

'What?' Darius asked.

'Sandra called me on Monday afternoon to ask about Moody's memorial service or burial or whatever you want to call it,' Danielle said.

'Moody had a burial?' Nihal asked in surprise. 'But I thought—'

'In India, a person who's been missing for seven years is presumed to be dead. When Moody's wallet and blood-covered clothes were found, somebody—probably the god-fearing grandmother in Goa—felt the need for a funeral. I attended because Sandra was teaching a semester at Northwestern in Chicago and couldn't attend herself. I quite enjoy the plangency of Sewri Cemetery. All those old tombstones with their forgotten tales about young women who died in shipwrecks and young men who died when their balloon burst, and—'

'Burst balloon,' we chorused. 'That was on a tombstone?'

'Patience, patience,' Danielle said, waving a cigarette and scattering ash over her purple lap. 'When she phoned me on Monday, Sandra wanted to know about the burial. Were the cousins there? Was the girlfriend there? Were the other friends there? And, more than anything else, where exactly in the cemetery had Moody been buried?'

'Do you know where Moody was buried?' Darius asked.

'Sewri Cemetery is vast. I'm not the sort to remember plot numbers and directions,' Danielle said. 'But I am the sort to remember poems and trivia. I recalled walking past the tomb of a young man who had died when his balloon burst. And a tomb which was topped by an open book made of marble. Once upon a time, there must have been a prayer or an epitaph inscribed on the book—but that had been erased by the winds and the loiterers.'

'A book without words,' Sunidhi and I squealed together.

'Precisely,' Danielle said, stopping for a sip of water before continuing. 'While Moody's service was taking place, I had plenty of time to look around. The tomb to my right had the words of "Remember" inscribed on it, which was a rather commonplace choice. More interesting was the tomb across the way: An elaborate affair with a stone pillar with a sort of wreath on top. It belonged to a young man who had been killed by a fall from a railway carriage at Calian Station. Which is, of course, Kalyan Station. I was struck by the coincidence. Moody was also a young man and Kalyan and Kasara are similar sorts of places.'

For a long minute, none of us breathed, moved or spoke. I don't know what the others were doing, but in my head, I was striking off items on a muddy, crumpled slip of paper with a red marker.

~~Burst balloon~~
~~Open book without words~~
~~Rossetti~~
~~Young man—train—Callian/ Calian~~

Fortunately, Sunidhi had the presence of mind to ask that most important question: 'But why did Sandra Saldanha want to know all this? Did she explain?'

Danielle sighed and shook her head angrily. 'Sandra wanted to find Moody's grave. She said something about having narrowed it down to three graves. She thought all of this—the marble book without words, the boy from Calian—would help her identify the precise grave.'

'But why?' Sunidhi asked again. 'Why did she want to find the grave?'

Danielle wiped her eyes and said in a wheezy, angry voice, 'Sandra was a fool. She should have left well alone.'

It was twenty minutes later, while we were stuck in traffic at Mahalakshmi, that we cracked the remaining clues.

SC stood for Sewri Cemetery. Of course.

And NW S 13? NE 6 A? N 10 J?

To me, at least, they sounded like the three graves that Sandra Saldanha had shortlisted.

An Aha Moment

Tuesday, May 9

My father was in a jokey mood during dinner. 'So,' he guffawed, 'I met Darius's father in the gym, and I hear that you and your friends are solving the murder of that poor swimming pool woman. Who are your chief suspects? They must be shivering in fear.'

I laughed weakly but didn't answer. Partly because my father would have been appalled to see our list of suspects. And partly because I was too distracted by the chant in my head.

Moody is in Sewri
But where oh where is D?

The rhyme plagued me while I brushed my teeth, shampooed my hair, straightened my room and collapsed onto my bed. I was all but asleep when another question tiptoed into my head: 'Moody is dead. But who is D?'

Suddenly, I was awake. And suddenly I knew.

I knew what linked Sandra Saldanha's death to the events of twenty-six years ago. I knew what Sandra Saldanha had meant when she talked about ghosts.

Sitting up, I grabbed my phone and sent a message on the Detective Club chat.

'Moody never returned from the hills near Kasara,' I typed, with fat fingers and a thumping heart. 'But D did. If he is still alive, where is he? And who is he? What is his new identity?'

My phone rang thirty seconds later, startling me so much that I yelped.

'Sorry for calling so late,' Nihal said when I answered. 'But I've been thinking the same thing.'

'That?'

'That if Dheeraj killed Moody, he must have created a new identity for himself. And if he did that, he could be anywhere...'

'...and anyone,' I whispered as I jumped out of bed, hurried across the dark room and pressed the switches with shaking fingers. Yellow light flooded the room, but it didn't banish the dark possibilities. And from the tremor in Nihal's voice, I knew he was afraid too.

'Maybe Sandra saw Dheeraj and recognized him. Maybe Dheeraj was the ghost from her past.'

'And maybe Dheeraj was afraid that Sandra Saldanha would go to the police and decided that the only way out was to kill Sandra Saldanha.'

As I paced up and down my room, I tried to tell myself that this was just a theory. An idea built out of a flimsy scrap of paper, a poem, half-remembered remarks. We could be wrong. Except that I knew that we were right. Sandra Saldanha had been killed by a ghost from her past. She had been killed by Dheeraj.

'What do we know about Dheeraj?' Nihal asked at that moment.

'He must be around forty-five years old. And a long time ago he was dull and bulky.'

'But if he managed to kill Moody, get hold of his money and then vanish without a trace...'

'...then he can't be all that dull,' I concluded as I pushed aside the window blind and peered at the tall silhouette of Maple Towers.

Dheeraj could be in there. Dheeraj could be anywhere.

Almost as if he was staring at the same silhouette and thinking the same thoughts that I was, Nihal whispered, 'Mr Kotecha, Dr Prabhu, Gurudev Mishr and Renato Sir are all around forty-five years old.'

'And Aarush Butalia,' I added. 'But listen, I think we are jumping to conclusions. Dheeraj could also be a complete stranger. He may not even be connected with The Orchard.'

'That's possible,' Nihal agreed. 'But there's a decent chance that he lives or works here.'

'Why?'

'Just think about it. Sandra Saldanha was sick and at home through most of April. The first time she stepped out of her apartment was on that Tuesday to attend yoga class. The first time she left The Orchard after her illness was to meet her friends at The Gymkhana on Saturday. But by then she was already afraid.'

'Which means she saw Dheeraj between Tuesday and Friday. Which means that she probably saw him in The Orchard.'

Nihal and I were still discussing this twenty minutes later when my father spotted the slit of yellow light under my bedroom door. He came in just as I was telling Nihal that I would make a timeline and that he should make a new list of suspects.

'Paromita, it's not healthy to keep thinking about murder,' my father scolded after I disconnected the call. 'Maybe this Detective Club was not such a good idea. Maybe we should travel after all...'

'I'm going to bed, I'm going to bed,' I said and lay down under my blue quilt. 'Good night.'

My father turned off the lights, ruffled my hair and left the room. Before allowing myself to fall asleep, I checked the phone one last time. There were two messages from Miss Rehana:

What is all this about Moody and D? I see I have some catching up to do

Prakash Sir will do a 10-minute call with you tomorrow at 3 p.m.

Happy it has worked out

I was happy too. We now had a working theory, a list of suspects and a call with the city's most famous detective. This was progress.

Timeline of Moody and D's Story

August 1997
Moody and D go trekking, disappear.

September 1997
Dheeraj's parents return from pilgrimage and realize he is missing.
Contact police.
Police start hunting in hills near Kasara but find nothing.
Police find bank accounts emptied.

Later in 1997
Dheeraj writes letters to parents telling them not to look for him.

August 1999
SS writes an article about the missing boys.
Talks about the devastating impact on the boys' friends and girlfriend.

2008/9

Trekker finds Moody's wallet and bloodied clothes in ditch.

Moody presumed dead and memorial service held for him.

Timeline of Events Leading to Murder

April 1 to April 24

SS has malaria. Doesn't leave the house.

Dr Prabhu visits her in mid-April. SS accuses him of malpractice.

Tuesday, April 25

SS attends first yoga class after illness.

Suspects Gurudev Mishr is fraud.

Mishr aggressive and jumpy.

Wednesday, April 26

Late-night soundchecks for Gauri Kotecha's wedding function.

SS goes downstairs to complain late at night.

Thursday, April 27

SS calls Vidya. Says she is so tired that she is seeing ghosts.

Friday, April 28
SS quiet and withdrawn during yoga.
Drops potted oregano near West Lawn.
Later says something like 'not a ghost after all'.
Locks and bolts her door as if afraid.

Saturday, April 29
Washing machine repaired.
SS meets Zarine, Danielle and Vidya at The Gymkhana.
Asks them if they remember Moody's real name.
SS hears noises outside door late at night, calls security.

Monday, May 1
SS calls library and borrows medical dictionary.
SS calls Danielle and asks about location of Moody's grave.
(Probably takes notes on the back of washing machine repair bill while Danielle talks about burst balloon, book without words...)
SS calls driver Gajanan Shinde and asks him to come to work by 8 a.m. on Tuesday.
(Was she planning to go to Sewri Cemetery to identify the grave? Had she already made one trip to the cemetery?)

Tuesday, May 2
SS killed at 8.17 a.m.

Observations:

SS mentioned ghosts on Thursday during call with Vidya and on Friday after yoga to Mrs Menon.

Possible that SS went down to complain late on Wednesday night, saw Dheeraj and thought her eyes were playing tricks on her.

On Friday after yoga, saw Dheeraj again and realized that she was right, after all.

Questions:

Why did SS borrow a medical dictionary the day before she died?

Why did she want to find Moody's grave?

Why was Dheeraj around so late on Wednesday night? Does he live or work here?

Plan of Action:

- Visit Sewri Cemetery.
- Contact Danielle and Vidya and ask for a better description of Dheeraj.
- Ask Prakash Talwar whether possible for someone to create an entirely new identity.

Visiting the Dead

Wednesday, May 10

None of us had heard of Sewri Cemetery before Tuesday evening—but by the time the Uber stopped outside the gate on Wednesday morning, we were pretty much world experts. Google had informed us that the cemetery started out as a European graveyard over 150 years ago, and that it housed 22,000 souls spread over 40 acres. It had also warned us that 40 acres was as big as 380 basketball courts.

None of us were thrilled about having to hunt for three graves scattered across 380 basketball courts in this boiling heat—but Darius was particularly grumpy. 'I would choose needle in a haystack any day,' he kept saying, till I wished I had a needle to jab into his thigh and then hide in a haystack.

This, though, was not the time to squabble. We needed our wits about us as we walked under the metal arch and into the sprawling city of the dead.

Sewri Cemetery was exactly what the horror movies had led us to expect: a grey and gloomy expanse of crumbling stone, dust and memories. Our footsteps were startling in the eerie silence and Darius' neon orange T-shirt screamed against that bleak greyness.

We could hardly blame the man in a khaki uniform who stepped out from a clump of tombstones and yelled in loud Marathi, 'Where are you going?'

Sunidhi—who had spent the entire Uber ride talking about a film called *Forget Me Not*—let out a bloodcurdling howl. This started Darius yowling. And then for some inexplicable reason, I decided that the khaki man was Dheeraj, and start shrieking loudest of all.

Mr Khaki waited for us to quieten down before making it clear that we were not welcome. 'Children are not allowed unless accompanied by an adult,' he said as he shooed us out of the cemetery and onto the pavement. So there we stood in a hot huddle, wondering how to find an adult who would be willing to spend the morning hunting for the graves of three strangers in a dusty, insect-filled cemetery.

None of our parents knew what we were up to. None of our drivers and didis and uncles and tuition teachers could be trusted to keep our secret. So now what?

'Let's hire someone like that coconut seller. I bet he would do it for Rs 500,' Darius was suggesting when I had my brainwave. 'I know, I know,' I exclaimed. 'Let me ask my Nani. She's the most sporting adult I know.'

It took two minutes to assure the others that Nani would not snitch to their parents. It took another four minutes to make the call and explain matters to Nani. It took thirty-three minutes for her to digest the information, wear a graveyard-appropriate kurta and make her way to Sewri Cemetery. And much sooner than we had hoped and Mr Khaki had expected, we were back amidst the stone angels and crumbling pyramids.

I felt much braver with Nani around. Nani was unfazed by the freshly dug graves, the reptilian, rustling sounds and the possibility of Gurudev Mishr/ Dr Prabhu lunging at us from behind a grieving angel. In fact, she was behaving pretty much as she would in the aisles of Nature's Basket. 'Now tell me what you're looking for,' she said, holding up a photocopy of Sandra Saldanha's jottings as if it was a grocery list.

'These,' Nihal said, pointing at NW S 13, NE 6 A and N 10 J. 'We think they are probably graves.'

'Whose graves?' Nani asked.

'One of them belongs to someone called Moody,' I said, realizing that this sounded odd.

Nani frowned, but all she said was, 'Okay. Let's start with NW S 13.'

Locating NW S 13 took time. The layout of the graveyard was confusing, the smaller paths were choked with weeds and rubble, and Nani and Sunidhi insisting on dawdling and discussing tombstones along the way.

Their favourite discovery was a tombstone that stated:

James Legath
Health Officer
Born at Seabank, old Aberdeen Scotland
Died at Seabank, Malabar Hill Bombay

Sunidhi said that she could tell that James Legath had been a happy man. Nani agreed and by the end I was feeling left out and crabby.

NW S 13 turned out to be a crumbling grave in a forlorn corner. Not even Nani and Sunidhi tried to loiter. And we all agreed that if there were ghosts in Sewri Cemetery, this is where they would congregate on a moonless night. (Or, for that matter, on a sun-dazzled morning.)

Thankfully, NE 6 A was located in a livelier section of the cemetery. We walked alongside two women carrying bunches of white flowers and found ourselves just a few graves away from a hunched man placing roses on a tombstone.

This particular section was higgly-piggly with tombs and we were tiptoeing around, feeling pretty hopeless when Sunidhi let out a yell. 'Look,' she said, pointing straight ahead.

We looked—and saw Sandra Saldanha's rough sketch come to life.

A marble pillar draped with marble flowers.

With pounding hearts and crossed fingers, we picked our way past dried grass and stones up to the tomb. And found ourselves staring at an epitaph which read: Here rests the remains of James Durrand who was killed at Calian Station by a fall from a railway carriage.

James Durand had been 19 when he died in 1875.

Moody had been 20 when he died in 1997.

Three graves away from Durrand's final resting place—right next to a tombstone inscribed with a verse from 'Remember'—was a flimsy black cross. Written on it in flaking gold was the name Morton Oswald D'Souza.

We had found Moody.

We'd reached the end of Sandra Saldanha's clue hunt but—standing under the vicious sun in that neglected graveyard—we felt let down and confused. There was no treasure here. No arrow pointing to Sandra Saldanha's killer. No hint about what Sandra Saldanha had hoped to find. Just a name, a date and a cross marking a tragedy.

'Are you done here?' Nani asked.

'Yes. Let's go. It's so hot,' I said, although I was suffocated, not by heat but by the despair emanating from that patch of earth.

'Yes, please let's go,' Sunidhi echoed, and I knew that she had felt it too.

The Pieces Refuse to Fit

Wednesday, May 10

Although eager to return to the realm of beating hearts and honking cars, we had one last stone to unturn before we left the cemetery.

The Sewri Cemetery office was a little shed near the gate. We hovered at the door while Nani marched inside and smiled at the manager. 'I'm sorry to disturb you,' she said. 'I was wondering, do you remember a woman who visited the cemetery around ten days ago? Her name was Sandra Saldanha.'

The manager, a bespectacled man named Mr Fonseca, jerked upright as if he had been jabbed with a sharp pencil. 'The same Sandra Saldanha who…?' he asked.

Nani nodded and said, 'The same Sandra Saldanha who…'

'I've been wondering,' Mr Fonseca exclaimed. 'But I thought it was too much of a coincidence.'

'So she did visit the cemetery?' Nani asked.

'Oh yes,' Mr Fonseca confirmed. 'She was very anxious to find the grave of that young man. She urgently needed to contact his family. Poor woman.'

Mr Fonseca tutted for some time, after which he supplied the details we needed. Sandra Saldanha had visited Sewri Cemetery last Monday. She had spent more than an hour leafing through the 2008 and 2009 registers in the office, had shortlisted three graves, copied out the addresses of the next of kin and said that she would be back the next day.

Of course, she had not returned.

Mr Fonseca hadn't given it much thought till a couple of days later when he turned on the TV and heard about a murder involving a college professor named Sandra Saldanha. 'I had a bad feeling,' he said mournfully. 'But then death waits around every corner. Nobody knows that better than me.'

Nani decided that it was time to wrap up this doleful conversation. And, for that matter, this grim expedition. She thanked Mr Fonseca, hurried us out of the cemetery, hydrated us with coconut water, herded us into her car and dropped us off at The Orchard.

Her stern expression boded badly for me. I tried my best to hop out of the car with the others but Nani gripped my wrist so tight that her ring bit into my skin. 'What's going on here?' she hissed. 'Does your father know about all this? I'm not—'

She was cut off mid-sentence by a gun-toting security guard who informed us that today was the Gauri Kotecha wedding and that outside cars were not allowed to stop in the complex. 'Move on, move on,' he shouted.

Gratefully, I did as I was told. But it took more than a gun-toting bully to defeat Nani. Even before I reached the elevator, my phone had pinged. 'Nana and I are coming tonight,' Nani had written. 'Will order dinner from Swati Snacks so won't be trouble for Meena. Am most interested to know why you risked sunstroke, snake bites and vampire bites to find grave of stranger.'

When put like that, our behaviour did appear odd. But not as odd as Sandra Saldanha's.

'Don't you think it's weird that Sandra Saldanha was looking for Moody's grave?' Sunidhi asked as we stepped into Apartment 492, hurried into my bedroom, turned on the AC and collapsed onto the blue rug. 'I mean, if she spotted Dheeraj after a gap of twenty-six years, she should have been shocked and scared. She should have gone to the police or put more locks on her door. But instead, she spent the whole time looking for Moody's grave. Why?'

'So that she could find Moody's cousins?' Darius shrugged. 'That's what the graveyard manager seemed to think.'

'But why?' Sunidhi repeated. 'How could Moody's cousins have helped her deal with Dheeraj?'

‘So then maybe the theory about Dheeraj is wrong,’ I admitted, and the others nodded gloomily.

The dust and disappointment clung to us through the afternoon. We barely ate the red sauce pasta that Meena didi served for lunch. We barely reacted when Dr Prabhu told us that we were no longer infectious. We even approached the call with Prakash Talwar with less enthusiasm than before. Our theory, which had seemed so clever till a few hours back, now seemed amateurish and fantastical.

Still, we prepped for the conversation and waited on my bedroom floor in an expectant circle. At exactly 3 p.m., Darius’s phone rang. After putting it on speaker, we placed it on the blue rug.

‘Rehana has been telling me about your exploits,’ Prakash Talwar started the conversation, sounding quite as imposing as he looked. ‘Now tell me what you’ve found so far.’

Darius had been nominated to do the talking. He related the story—except the bits where we had disobeyed Miss Rehana. He began with Nihal’s discovery of the crumpled paper and ended with the tale of Moody and D. ‘We figured that the paper was related to these two boys who disappeared in 1997 while they went on a trek,’ he concluded. ‘It looks like Dheeraj murdered Moody. We think that Sandra Saldanha spotted Dheeraj, who then decided to kill her.’

Prakash Talwar greeted the story with a prolonged and puzzled silence. 'But the words on that paper?' he asked eventually. 'Did you decipher them?'

'Yes. They led us to a particular grave in Sewri Cemetery.'

'Whose grave?'

'Moody's grave,' Darius explained.

'I see,' Prakash Talwar said, sounding even more befuddled. 'But how does this D'Souza chap's grave connect with the murder? Even if Sandra Saldanha recognized this Dheeraj person, why was she looking for Morton D'Souza's grave? And do you have any idea about this Dheeraj's new identity?'

'No,' Darius admitted. 'But we have a bunch of suspects.'

Prakash Talwar was silent for another long spell, and we could hear loud bangs and bursts of Bollywood music in the background. Then finally he spoke. 'It's a fascinating theory and would make a great Netflix serial. But the sad thing about real-life crimes—especially murders—is that they are usually boring affairs that are committed because of anger or greed. The most tedious emotions. Now, can I trust you?'

'Yes,' we chorused.

'I'm telling you this in the strictest confidence, but that poor woman had lent some money to someone. And when she asked for it to be repaid, the person decided to kill her. I'm positive about the identity of the killer. What I'm now looking for is proof.'

'Oh okay,' we mumbled. 'So you've solved the murder…'

You didn't need to be a detective to know that we were crushed. Prakash Talwar sensed this and tried to cheer us up. 'Even though you arrived at the wrong conclusion, I'm amazed by your detective work,' he said. 'I have a suggestion. Why don't you children come to my office for a few days next month. You can watch us work, and we can talk about all that goes into an investigation.'

The detective's words had the desired effect. We unslumped and ungloomed. We told him that we would love to intern with him and grinned at each other.

'Excellent,' Prakash Talwar said. 'I'll get Rehana to set it up.'

The great detective ended the call before we could get to our questions, but we could always ask when we interned with him.

Too Much Blood

Wednesday, May 10

At 6 o'clock on Wednesday evening, a shehnai started wailing on the West Lawn. The Gauri Kotecha wedding was about to begin.

The shehnai—which was loud enough to wake James Legath, James Durrand and friends from their eternal slumber—put me in a foul mood. The wedding security put Nani, Nana, my father and the Swati Snacks delivery boy in an even fouler mood.

My father was enraged because he had been treated like a 'common criminal' and made to fill a form to enter his own home. Nana was livid because the Swati Snacks delivery boy had been kept waiting outside. 'The panki must be soggy,' he grumbled. 'The khichdi must be cold. Let's eat quickly.'

Nana is capable of week-long sulks over melted kulfi, so we all hurried to the table. This meant that I was unable to warn Nani that my father knew nothing about the Sewri Cemetery expedition and almost nothing about the Sandra Saldanha investigation. Still, I hoped that the Kotecha wedding would occupy us through dinner.

For the first half of the meal, Meena didi regaled us with wedding trivia. She told us that the reception had a fairytale theme and that the West Lawn had been done up with 18,000 crystal stars and 100 kg of white roses. A Disney-style castle had been erected to serve as a stage for Deepika Padukone and Ranveer Singh.

Nani, though, is not an easily distractable person. The moment Meena didi paused, she turned to me and said, 'Okay, Paromita. What was going on at the cemetery? Who is this Moody boy? How does it connect with the murder of Sandra Saldanha? I hope you aren't taking silly risks.'

My father and Nana frowned.

'What silly risks?' Nana asked.

'What cemetery?' my father demanded.

'Nothing, nothing. It was just something I did with the Detective Club,' I said airily to my father before turning to Nani. 'We were just testing theories, and our theory turned out to be wrong.'

'Hmmm okay,' Nani said in her let-me-be-the-judge-of-that voice. 'Why don't you tell us anyway?'

'There's been so much drama,' Meena didi jumped in gleefully. 'Thieves in Paromita's bedroom breaking cows. The children running here, running there in Ubers.'

'What?' the other adults went off like the Kotecha firecrackers. 'Ubers? Thieves?'

Left with no option, I started speaking. I had barely got to the missing scrap of paper and our initial list of suspects when my father freaked. 'Paromita,' he burst out, 'I don't know what to say...you children...suspecting the doctor...suspecting Aarti's brother...you've crossed limits...I'm sorry I encouraged this club...I really think it's time to wrap it up.'

'It's probably going to wrap up anyway,' I said. 'Prakash Talwar, who is a very famous detective, is now investigating Sandra Saldanha's murder. And we no longer have chicken pox so there's no real need for the club.'

'Good,' Nani said. 'But tell me, who was that boy in the cemetery?'

Once again left with no option, I related the tale of Moody and D. My audience was transfixed and even Meena didi, who'd been flitting from window to window, hoping to catch a glimpse of the wedding, stopped to listen.

'So that poor boy was an orphan and was killed by his own friend?' she exhaled when I was done. 'Some people are born unlucky.'

'Moody was unlucky in many ways,' I agreed. 'He had an illness where you bleed and bleed even if you get a small cut or scratch.'

'Oh, yes,' Nani said, turning to Nana. 'Vandana's son has it. Do you remember the time they came for dinner, and he cut his finger and bled all over the Istanbul rug? It was so frightening. And the stain never went fully.'

There was a pause in the conversation, while we returned to our neglected pankis and puris. Which was when Meena didi uttered the words that cracked open the case.

'Just like that supervisor,' she sniffed. 'He just wouldn't stop bleeding.'

'What?' I asked, thinking I had misheard.

'The pest control supervisor who came on Sunday,' Meena didi elaborated. 'He went around the house to check things and he must have cut his finger. You should have seen the blood. As it is, he looked half dead. All crooked and limping as if someone had beaten him up. I gave him ice and told him to sit on the sofa. There's still a stain there. Look.'

The hairs on my arms stood on end as I gazed at a spot of brown, easy to miss on the moss green, raw-silk upholstery. Another memory tickled me. Of another spot of dark brown that could easily have been overlooked.

In my dressing table drawer.

Around me the adults talked about weddings and stomach bugs. I heard very little. I was thinking about blood.

About Moody, who had haemophilia and had bled so much that he sometimes needed to be driven to hospital.

About a Pest O Kill supervisor who was here on the day that Sandra Saldanha's paper was stolen. And who had bled on the sofa and on the living room floor. And perhaps into a dressing table drawer which had been used to store a vital clue.

About two lines in a poem that could mean many things. 'Oozing blood. Oozing death.'

About a medical dictionary that had been borrowed a day before a murder.

There was too much blood in this story. And it was not a coincidence.

A few days before she died, Sandra Saldanha had seen a ghost from her past. We'd been right about that.

What we'd been wrong about was the identity of the ghost. The person she had seen was not Dheeraj.

It was Moody.

The Forces of Evil Gather

Wednesday, May 10

The moment my grandparents left, I rushed to my computer and pulled up the article that Sandra Saldanha had written in 1999 about the two missing boys. The first time I'd skimmed through it and hadn't bothered with the details. This time I read it with careful attention.

Sandra Saldanha had described one of the boys as good-hearted, always happy to help carry parcels and to treat friends to a round of fried rice or a late-night show of *Yes Boss*.

This sounded like Dheeraj.

She had described the other boy who—although he dealt with unimaginable health problems and had no close family barring a grandmother in Mapusa—possessed charm and quicksilver intelligence. His disappearance had left his friends bereft, and his girlfriend unable to dance or study or even return to college.

This was certainly Moody.

I wondered briefly if we should try to find the girlfriend. But locating a girl named Rina or Radha after a gap of twenty-six years seemed almost impossible. So, putting aside the idea, I turned to the Detective Club chat and asked the question that had been bothering me.

'Nihal,' I wrote, 'was there a bookmark in the medical dictionary?'

'Yes,' Nihal replied after a short interval.

'Do you remember the pages it marked?' I typed with a pounding heart.

'No,' Nihal replied.

Before I could feel too crushed, a second message flashed on the screen: 'Wait. I think I sent my mother a picture of the pages.'

Seconds later, a photograph arrived. I clicked on it, peered at the contents, and jumped with excitement. Actually.

Sandra Saldanha had stuck a square of pink paper in the medical dictionary to mark diseases beginning with H. Hand-Foot-and-Mouth Disease. Hantavirus. Hepatitis A.

And Haemophilia.

The pieces of the puzzle had clicked into place.

The beeping of my phone yanked me back to the here and now. The Detective Club chat was buzzing.

Nihal: Why are you asking about the medical dictionary?

Sunidhi: Have you thought of something?

Miss Rehana: Prakash Sir says the case is almost solved. Should we have a final meeting tomorrow? Request you not to say or do anything that can confuse the situation.

Darius: Stop teasing

I typed my response with shaking fingers. 'I've figured something out.'

'What? What? Tell!!!!!' Sunidhi demanded.

'We've been looking at things from the wrong end,' I replied.

'Stop being so vague,' Darius ranted. 'Tell NOW.'

'Tomorrow morning. When you come over,' I messaged back, before putting my phone face down on the bed, heading to my desk and getting down to work.

First, I read my notes.

Second, I wrote down all that we knew about Moody.

Third, I messaged Zarine and asked if she, Danielle and Vidya could send us a detailed description of Moody. Anything that popped into their heads. (Their responses came within half an hour. Slight, nice looking, charming, impressive talker. May have walked with a limp. Fragile. Unwell a lot of the time.)

Fourth, I asked Meena didi about the Pest O Kill supervisor. (Short and thin. Limped and a bit hunched. He looked like he'd been in an accident.)

Fifth, I read up on haemophilia and found that episodes of bleeding in joints and muscles can cause arthritis, chronic pain, a hunched posture, difficulty in walking and movement.

Sixth, I figure what I knew and what I didn't.

This is what I knew: that if Moody had come into the house disguised as a pest control supervisor on Sunday morning, then he was not Mr Kotecha, Dr Prabhu, Renato, Gurudev Mishr or Aarush Butalia. Meena didi knew all these people and was not likely to be fooled by a black Pest O Kill shirt.

This is what I didn't know: Who was Moody? Why had he been on the West Lawn so late on Wednesday night when Sandra Saldanha had gone down to complain? How had he known about the scrap of paper in my dressing table drawer? How had he known that the pest control people were going to land up here? And how had he so successfully camouflaged himself as one of them?

I didn't have answers, but the questions were useful. As I turned them over in my head, I realized two things:

Moody was associated with The Orchard in some way.

And Moody had a peephole into The Chicken Pox Club.

Which meant that Moody could well be somebody we knew. Somebody who was a part of our world. Ugly though the idea was, I forced myself to look at it in the face and examine the possibilities.

Darius's father? No, he was built like a wrestler, ran the marathon and could never have disguised himself as a hunched pest control supervisor.

Sunidhi's father? No, Sandra Saldanha had known him for years. She wouldn't have waited all this time to discover that he was Moody.

Nihal's father? No, he'd been in Canada for the past month.

I thought about the drivers who worked for us. Of Meena didi and Tiwariji. Of the teachers conducting Summer Selebration workshops.

And then I thought of Miss Rehana.

Miss Rehana, who was on the Detective Club chat. Who had been in the room when I put the scrap of paper in the drawer. Who had a capacity for blazing anger. Who had tried to stop us from meeting Sandra Saldanha's friends and often seemed to be blocking our investigations rather than encouraging them.

What did Miss Rehana know about us?

Quite a lot. She knew where we lived. She knew about our families. She knew what we were saying on the chat. She knew that I had figured out something important.

What did we know about Miss Rehana?

Nothing.

It was at that moment that, on the West Lawn, a hundred fireworks exploded.

In my bedroom, my phone pinged, and the screen lit up with a notification. I glanced at the phone without interest when my eyes snagged on a name. A name that could not be there. A name that felt like a punch to the chest.

My eyes were playing tricks, of course. But still I had to look.

Picking up my phone, I stared at the screen. Somewhere from a great distance, I could hear Meena didi. Telling me to have the peppermint tea while it was hot. Asking me if something was the matter. Her words were drowned by the slamming of my heart. And the screaming in my head.

Sitting in my phone was a message from Sandra Saldanha.

Time to Fight Back

Wednesday, May 10

For a dizzying moment I thought Sandra Saldanha was back. Standing in her balcony against the floodlit sky while 'Deewani Mastani' played at top volume and 2000 people whistled and screamed. Waiting with a bloody smile.

Then the music died down. The brown haze in my head receded. And I knew that the message waiting in my phone was not from a dead woman. It was from the person who had grabbed Sandra Saldanha's phone before fleeing her apartment.

It was a message from Sandra Saldanha's killer.

This is what the message said:

Your Nani goes for a morning walk to Worli Seaface

Sunidhi's mother works in Bandra

Your father works late

So many things can go wrong

So many people don't come back home

I know where to find you. You don't know where to find me

Best you stop now

As I stared at the phone screen, I knew that this wasn't an empty threat. Moody had killed at least twice. He would kill again if necessary.

Moody was feeling cornered. My message on the Detective Cub chat had rattled him. For the moment, he was trying to scare us into silence. But soon he would be looking for permanent solutions. As long as Moody was out and about, we were in danger. We would be afraid to open the front door, to step into the swimming pool, to leave the complex.

The only way we could ever be safe was to unmask Morton Oswald D'Souza.

But how?

I needed advice, but who could I ask?

Not my father. Not Nani. Certainly not Miss Rehana.

After stumbling around my room for a few minutes, I picked up *The Detective's Bible*, turned automatically to the first page and stared at it with tired, unfocused eyes. There was only one sentence on the page and, at first, it shivered and blurred, as if the book was lying at the bottom of a swimming pool. But slowly I found myself staring at four words written in a large, bold font: **Leave no stone unturned.**

As I sat on the sofa with a banging heart and rubbery finger, it struck me that there was one stone that I had left unturned. My English teacher, Miss Pavri.

Miss Pavri must have been a student at St Paul's College at around the same time as Moody and D. There was a chance that she had known them—or at least known of them.

No matter how awkward it was to message a teacher at 11.21 p.m. in the middle of the summer holidays, I had to try. And so, picking up my phone and swallowing my embarrassment, I typed:

> So sorry to disturb you, Miss Pavri, but I needed to check something with you. I don't know if I ever mentioned it, but Sandra Saldanha used to be my neighbour. I bought her book of poems recently and came across a poem called "Moody and D" about two boys who disappeared while on a trek. I became curious about them and started doing some research. Was just wondering if you knew Moody and Dheeraj or any details about what happened to them.

Miss Pavri would not respond at this hour of the night. Maybe she'd get so irritated that she would not respond at all. Still, I pressed Send.

Then, because I could no longer bear to sit around with chattering teeth while blue and pink fireworks shredded the sky outside my window, I began to write notes in my HDFC diary. As I wrote, I started paying attention to the sequence of recent events.

At 9.34 p.m., I had asked Nihal about the medical dictionary.

At 9.47 p.m., I'd said, 'I've figured something out. Something important. We've been looking at things from the wrong end.'

At 11.15 p.m., the killer had used Sandra Saldanha's phone to send a threatening message.

There was no doubt that Moody was eavesdropping on the Detective Club chat. There was no doubt that Miss Rehana was passing on the messages to him or...

Grabbing my phone, I checked the Detective Club chat and counted six participants: Darius, Nihal, Sunidhi, me, Rehana and Rehana-Talwar Kumar Investigations.

A chill entered my heart.

Could it be that one of the phones sat in Miss Rehana's mirrorwork bag, while the other phone sat in the hands of a man with an ugly secret? I imagined a shadowy figure in a dimly lit room, monitoring our every move. Who, even at this moment, was checking our chat to find out if we were getting any closer.

Till this moment, our adversary had known everything we knew and everything we planned to do. But no longer.

In the West Lawn, the music swelled, and the MC shouted, 'Are you ready?'

Taking a deep breath, I replied, 'I am.'

A Plan Is Hatched

Thursday, May 11

Darius, Nihal and Sunidhi were all awake and all happy to chat—even though it was 11.45 p.m. 'Thank God you set up this call,' Sunidhi cried. 'There's no way I'd have been able to sleep. What with the wedding and the mystery and everything. What do you mean, we've been looking at this from the wrong end? Tell!'

So that is what I did.

There was a stunned silence when I finished speaking, after which the others exploded into a noisy jumble.

...the pest control supervisor...I was always suspicious of the pest control people...wonder why Sandra Saldanha opened the door for Moody...if he is so hunched and weak, how did he manage to throw Sandra Saldanha from the balcony...refuse to believe that Miss Rehana is a villain...only way we can ever feel safe again is if Moody is caught...

Gradually, everyone ran out of things to say. And it was in that uneasy pause that Sunidhi demanded, 'What should we do? I can't think of a single idea.'

Neither could I, which is why I was relieved when Darius broke the silence. 'It sounds like Moody is panicking. If we push him a little, maybe he will dig his own grave...'

'Push him how?' Sunidhi asked.

'I have a plan,' Darius said slowly. 'It's not the greatest, but still.'

Darius was right. His plan was not the greatest. It was more Famous Five than Sherlock Holmes, but it was still worth a try. We spent some time discussing the details before we ended the call.

Minutes later, the Detective Club chat burst into life.

Nihal:
Zarine messaged
She thinks she knows where Sandra might have hidden the photograph

Sunidhi:
The one she was going to show the police?
The one of that group of students?
Where?

Nihal:
In SS's apartment

In some cardboard box
Zarine meeting us in Maple Towers lobby at 10 a.m. tomorrow

Darius:
I'm on

Sunidhi:
Me too

Paromita:
Didn't we agree that we should stop with the investigation?
It's getting too much and anyway my chess class is starting tomorrow

Sunidhi:
Let's just see if the photograph is there. If we find it, the police will be able to identify the killer and we'll have solved the case. If we don't find it, we just stop.

Nihal:
Makes sense
I hope we find the picture

Once the Detective Club chat quietened down, I waylaid my father, who was hunting for earplugs and grumbling about early meetings and noisy weddings. 'Can I go to Maple Towers for a short time?' I wheedled. 'Sunidhi's mother has made dessert for us. And none of us can sleep because of the noise. I'll carry the key, so I don't disturb anyone.'

My father agreed. Then once he disappeared into his bedroom, I crept into the balcony and stared at Maple Towers through the bright and noisy night. For a long time, nothing happened. Then my phone pinged. I assumed it was Nihal or Darius with an update—but no, it was Miss Pavri.

Miss Pavri had sent a long message:

Hi Paromita. Didn't realize you knew Sandra Saldanha. She was my favourite teacher and am still reeling. Just bought her book on Amazon. Thank you for telling me about it.

Moody and Dheeraj. Haven't thought about them in years. I hardly knew them, but my sister was in the same class and quite friendly with that gang. Especially with Ami, who was on the cover of a big science magazine recently.

I remember almost nothing about Dheeraj.

But there was always talk about Moody. He and Reena were both big spenders and kept borrowing money. There were rumours that Reena had skimmed money off the Canteen Committee. But that may have been pure cattiness because people were envious of Reena Kumar. She was in a couple of ads. She had these amazing light eyes and danced fabulously. But my sister always said that she had a way of looking at you which made you feel like a squashed bug. Ami was much gentler. I think she was dating a boy named Vikram.

But wait. You asked about Moody. He was very charming and played the sympathy card because he was frail and an orphan. But always unsavoury stories floating about how he used people shamelessly. Apparently, he befriended other students who were rich and extracted gifts and money. But can't remember specifics. Will ask my sister tomorrow morning.

Sorry haven't been of much help. Hope you are having a restful holiday.

I read the messages twice but there was nothing useful. Disappointed, I continued to stare into the night. And then suddenly, a window on the 56th floor of Maple Towers flashed with light. Once, then again. As if someone was walking around Sandra Saldanha's bedroom with a torch.

Moody/Miss Rehana had taken the bait.

Jumping to my feet, I sent a message and hurried out of the apartment.

We Meet a Killer

Thursday, May 11

Nihal and Darius were lurking in the shadows near Maple Towers, and we walked into the building together without exchanging a word. The security guard at the desk—Tiwariji? Bhonsaleji?—didn't seem to think it strange that three children should visit a friend well after midnight.

Darius, Nihal and I stepped into the elevator and made our way to the 54th floor. Sunidhi was waiting outside her apartment and, again without a word, we climbed the stairs to the 56th floor. This was where Gajanan Shinde had stood just nine days ago, ringing the doorbell, and wondering why Sandra Saldanha wasn't responding.

Unlike Gajanan Shinde, we didn't ring the doorbell. We crept past the doors of Apartment 561 and 562 and started climbing the stairs towards the 57th floor. Then we stopped midway and stood in a nervous clump, while Nihal sent his message on the Detective Chat:

Plans changed. Sorry

Danielle thinks SS moved the box with pic to Gymkhana locker

Meeting at Gymkhana tomorrow at 11 a.m.

I imagined a shadowy figure tiptoeing around Sandra Saldanha's dark apartment, looking for a cardboard box and an incriminating photograph—and a phone lighting up with this new message. How would Moody/ Miss Rehana react? Would they believe the message? Or would they start to suspect that they were being manipulated?

'I'm worried that they will suspect something,' I whispered to the others in that bright, silent, stairwell that smelt of lemon-scented soap.

'They've believed us so far,' Darius whispered back.

'You think they're both in there?' Sunidhi asked. 'But I just can't believe that Miss Rehana is evil. I can't understand why she would help Moody."

'What I can't understand is why Sandra Saldanha opened the door and allowed Moody into the house that morning,' Darius muttered. 'And if Moody is all that weak and limping, how could he have pushed Sandra Saldanha off the balcony. Maybe we are wrong—'

'We'll soon know,' Nihal mumbled before we lapsed into a nervous silence.

We hadn't expected our plan to work this far, and we weren't sure what to do next. Should we try to catch a glimpse of the person emerging from Apartment 562? Should we be doing something more—something like taking a photograph or pouncing on them?

'If it's just one person,' Darius whispered, 'I can try a football tackle.'

'Darius,' I pleaded under my breath, 'these are danger—'

I gulped and pressed my lips together. On the West Lawn, the music had stopped. On the 56th floor of Maple Towers, a door had opened.

Inching forward, we craned our necks and caught a glimpse of a figure dressed in something pink, flowy and glittery. A woman.

Miss Rehana. It had to be Miss Rehana.

The figure stepped out of the apartment, shut the door with the softest click and then stood at the landing. I assumed Miss Rehana was waiting for the elevator, but she stood very still and then turned and walked towards the flight of stairs heading downwards.

We could hear the clack of heels receding. Then silence.

When the footsteps started again, they were different. This time they were climbing up, getting louder, coming closer. I was wheezy with terror and next to me I could hear Sunidhi's breath catch.

Then the figure was back on the landing of the 56th floor and walking swiftly towards the section of the staircase that led upwards. The section where we were standing in a heart-thumping huddle. There was no time to react.

The woman in pink took one step. Then another. Then she turned the corner and stood staring straight up at us with pale grey eyes.

I gaped and thought, 'Who—?'

This woman was not Miss Rehana. She was someone else. Someone I had seen but couldn't place till Sunidhi yelped, 'Miss Heena, what are you doing here?'

The dance teacher took two steps towards us and examined us with those empty grey eyes. 'You stupid children,' she whispered as her hand darted into the folds of her flowy kurta.

'Gun,' someone said in the background.

Somebody else whimpered. I think it was me.

Sunidhi, though, seemed happy to catch up with her teacher—even if the circumstances were unusual. 'Miss Heena,' she cried. 'I've been practising the Butterfly Leap again and again. And I don't think my legs are too short, after all.'

Miss Heena was distracted for less than a heartbeat. But it was enough for Sunidhi. Flinging her arms and kicking her legs—quite a risky operation on that staircase—Sunidhi launched into a Butterfly Leap. The leap may not have been good enough for Miss Heena the dance teacher, but it was good enough for Miss Heena the midnight prowler.

Sunidhi sailed through the air and crashed loudly and dramatically into the woman in pink.

They both tumbled in an ungainly heap. A small black gun clattered onto the floor. Darius grabbed it and pulled Sunidhi up. Nihal and I stood guard over Miss Heena, who was groaning with pain and clutching her golden-sandalled foot.

Sunidhi called her father and asked him to hurry to the 56th floor. We would have called Tiwariji next, but a bald man living in Apartment 561 did it for us, moaning all the while, 'Are we to have no peace? Is somebody else getting murdered? This is too much.'

Sunidhi's father arrived a few minutes later, looking confused. He looked even more confused when he saw a woman in a glimmering pink salwar kameez sitting on the floor, shrieking at us, 'Thanks to you, a killer is on the loose.'

It bothered me that Miss Heena seemed angry rather than afraid. Given that she had been caught red-handed, emerging from the locked house of a murder victim, why wasn't she more panicked?

We got our answer thirty seconds later when Tiwariji and Bhonsleji burst out of the elevator and rushed to her. Instead of trying to nab her, they helped her to her feet and bleated, 'Sorry madam, sorry madam. Should we call the doctor? Did someone attack you? Should we call the police?'

As the security guards began to help the woman towards the waiting elevator, Darius yelled, 'What are you doing? This woman killed Sandra Saldanha.'

Tiwariji and Bhonsleji goggled at us with horrified expressions. 'Madam Kumar is in charge of the security of the building,' Tiwariji finally managed to say. 'She is a famous security expert.'

'I am one of the partners in Talwar Kumar Investigations,' Miss Heena/Madam Kumar flung over her zari-encrusted shoulder. 'You must be the children who formed that club with that half-witted Rehana. Well, thanks to you a killer has gotten away. And if my foot is fractured, you will pay a heavy price.'

'I'm so sorry, Miss Heena,' Sunidhi wailed, while her father echoed the apology in the background.

Miss Heena, though, was not one to accept apologies gracefully. Which proved to be her undoing. As she stepped into the lift, she wrinkled her nose and looked at us as if we were cockroaches.

And something clicked.

'She had these amazing light eyes and danced fabulously. But my sister always said that she had a way of looking at you which made you feel like a squashed bug.' Miss Pavri's words rang in my head like a fire-engine bell. Urgent and loud.

Miss Pavri had been talking about a girl named Reena Kumar. Who had light eyes. Who was a dancer. And who was Moody's girlfriend.

The woman standing in front of us had light eyes. She knew enough dance to pose as a dance teacher. And she was enmeshed in a case involving Moody. It felt like too much of a coincidence.

The woman in pink had just stepped into the elevator when I cried, 'Reena Kumar...student at St Paul's College. Moody's girlfriend. You helped Moody to disappear after he killed Dheeraj. Maybe you helped to kill Dheeraj as well. And you killed Sandra Saldanha...'

'You can't talk to Kumar Madam like this,' Tiwariji protested. And I could hear Sunidhi's father trying to shush me as well.

'Such nonsense,' the woman barked as she gestured to Darius. 'Give me my gun. Now.'

'Don't,' I started to say, but Bhonsleji snatched the gun from Darius, hurried towards the elevator to hand it over and managed to drop it on the way. He was fumbling for the gun when I screamed out the big question.

'Where is Moody?'

'What?' the woman snarled, gesturing angrily at Bhonsleji who was still gathering the gun and himself. 'How should I know?'

'You should know,' Nihal said softly. 'Because Moody is your partner in the detective agency. Moody is Prakash Talwar.'

Reena Kumar—because the rage on her face left no doubt that it was her—forgot about her gun and slammed the buttons on the lift. The doors started to shut in the slow way of elevators, which allowed us to see her expression disintegrate into evil.

'She's getting away,' Darius yelled, as the lift doors shut completely. But Tiwariji was already on his walkie talkie, giving instructions to the other security guards. And Sunidhi was congratulating Bhonsleji for the clever way in which he had dropped the gun and delayed Kumar Madam. (I still don't know if Bhonsleji was clever or clumsy. But he got a Kotecha Champion medal anyway.)

Sunidhi's mother phoned the policeman who had visited her a week ago, and told him there was an emergency. We waited in Sunidhi's house till 2 a.m., when a policeman came to tell us that Reena Kumar/ Kumar Madam/Miss Heena had been caught while trying to leave Maple Towers.

Moody/Prakash Talwar/the pest control supervisor had been nabbed in the security control room that had been set up for the wedding.

It was while we were waiting for news that I asked Nihal how he'd figured that Moody was Prakash Talwar.

'You didn't notice?' Nihal asked.

'Notice what?'

'When we had our chat with Prakash Talwar, we never once mentioned Moody's real name. But Prakash Talwar kept referring to him as "that Morton D'Souza chap". I wondered if I was imagining things, but when you figured that one of the partners of Talwar Kumar Investigations was Moody's girlfriend, it made sense that the other partner was Moody.'

'Amazing deduction,' I said.

'You identifying Reena Kumar was pretty amazing too,' Nihal said. 'And Sunidhi's Butterfly Leap probably saved our lives.'

'And,' I said a bit reluctantly, 'Darius's plan worked brilliantly.'

Back to Normal

You'd think the adults would give us a Zara coupon or at least a pat on the back for our nifty detective work. After all, we'd unmasked a cold-blooded killer.

But no. All they talked about was the gun that Reena Kumar had been carrying and the fact that we'd been reckless and foolhardy.

Even so, we were The Orchard celebrities for two days. Then Gracy Joseph, who had starred in a rather scandalous Netflix serial, moved into Gulmohar Towers and stole the limelight.

It was satisfying to know that we'd been right about many things. Moody had befriended Dheeraj for his wealth. Lumbering, unpopular Dheeraj had reciprocated with joy and generosity. But Moody wanted more—and decided to empty Dheeraj's bank accounts, kill him, and vanish with the money.

After the murder, Moody was careful to leave evidence indicating that he himself was dead. Dheeraj's childish handwriting was easy to copy, and Moody used it to send the note to Dheeraj's parents. He then moved to Indore, where he lived under an assumed name. Reena Kumar joined him and they ran a dance academy and an array of dubious businesses. Then in 2011, there was trouble with the police in Indore and the two of them vanished.

Three months later, 'Talwar Kumar Investigations' was launched in Mumbai.

Things were going swimmingly till two weeks ago, when Moody/Prakash Talwar—who was busy vetting the West Lawn for the Kotecha wedding late one night—looked up and saw Sandra Saldanha. She was staring at him with shocked recognition.

In that single moment, Sandra Saldanha's fate was sealed. The next day, Dance Monkeys were told that they would not be a part of Summer Selebrations this year—and a dance teacher named Miss Heena was appointed in their place.

Heena was, of course, Reena Kumar under an assumed name.

It was the perfect solution. As far as the residents of The Orchard were concerned, Miss Heena was the in-house dance teacher. As far as the security guards were concerned, Madam Kumar was checking The Orchard for security risks. As far as Miss Rehana was concerned, Reena Kumar was pretending to be a dance teacher to better monitor the security for the wedding.

Once she was ensconced in The Orchard, Reena Kumar started tailing her quarry. She followed Sandra

Saldanha to Sewri Cemetery on Monday and realized that the English professor was on the right track.

On Tuesday morning, Reena Kumar rang the doorbell of Apartment 562, Maple Towers. Sandra Saldanha—who was on the lookout for Moody—peered through the peephole, saw a woman standing outside, and opened the door.

She paid for this mistake with her life.

The one thing we'd been wrong about was Miss Rehana, who had not been involved in any way. She visited us two days after the midnight drama, looking sad and apologetic. 'I really had no idea that Prakash Sir was using the second phone to spy on you,' she said. 'I'm so, so sorry. And there were times when I thought you were messing the investigation and freaked at you. I'm sorry about that as well. The thing is, I was so eager to make a good impression on Prakash Talwar that I stopped thinking straight.'

We tried to cheer Miss Rehana by telling her that now that Mumbai had lost its foremost detective, there was a vacancy for her to fill. 'If you set up an agency we insist on interning with you,' Sunidhi said. 'And we promise not to suspect you again.'

Finally, Miss Rehana smiled.

Zarine, Danielle and Vidya invited us to The Gymkhana for a thank you lunch. We were quick to order watermelon juice before Zarine could order

Limca for us. Dessert was carrot cake, which was Sandra Saldanha's favourite food in the whole world.

Sandra Saldanha's friends raised a toast with forkfuls of cake. 'You were a fool Sandra,' Danielle said. 'But you were clever too. Thank you for leaving the clues behind for these rather remarkable children to find.'

I was thrilled that Danielle thought we were rather remarkable.

On Tuesday—a fortnight from the day that Sandra Saldanha was murdered—we went out for lunch to The Nutcracker. It was meant to be a celebration, but I wasn't feeling celebratory. Darius was leaving that evening for a horse-riding camp. Nihal was leaving for London in a few days and Sunidhi and her family were going to Mahabaleshwar for a week. This felt like the end of an adventure.

'So,' I said as we dug into our waffles, 'I guess this is the last meeting of the Chicken Pox Club.'

'Why?' Sunidhi asked.

'Because we no longer have chicken pox, we no longer have a mystery to solve, and everyone is travelling.'

'But everyone will be coming back,' Nihal said. 'And we can always look for a new mystery. Miss Rehana has promised to send some mysteries our way. I, at least, plan to remain a member of the Chicken Pox Club. Though I wouldn't mind if we changed the name to something less diseased.'

We spent the rest of the meal discussing alternate names. Sunidhi liked The Orchard Owls and Sugar Solutions. Darius was in favour of The Tower Rangers. Nihal and I played around with The Parel PIs. We didn't reach any decision so, for the moment at least, I guess we are still the Chicken Pox Club. (Which, if nothing else, is more dignified than Sugar Solutions!)

Back home, I bought Book No. 24. (*The Giver*. You must read it.)

I was deep in the story when my father phoned. 'Sunidhi's mother just called to ask if you can go to Mahabaleshwar with them,' he announced. 'What should I say?'

'Ummm, let me think about it,' I said.

'You don't want to go?' my father asked, sounding astonished. 'I thought you'd be somersaulting with joy.'

'I'll just call you back,' I said and hung up.

The thing is, I really, really wanted to go to Mahabaleshwar, but I wasn't sure that Sunidhi wanted me to go. A bunch of her cool-girl friends were also heading there, and I suspected that I'd only been invited because kind Mrs Menon was sorry for me.

I was still walking up and down my room, wondering what to do, when my phone rang and Sunidhi yelled into my ear, 'Paromita, you are coming, right? Please, please do. We will have such fun and maybe we will even find a mystery. And we can share a room and I will show you my favourite cake shop and there is delicious porridge for breakfast and...'

'I'm coming,' I laughed.

When I hung up, I decided that this was officially the best summer ever. One case solved. Two and a half new friends made. One hundred and twenty-five books. And a week in Mahabaleshwar. All that was needed to make life perfect was the news that Aarti Butalia was moving to Ulaanbaatar.

I was too excited to return to *The Giver*, so I tidied my room instead. I placed the HDFC diary in a drawer after checking that there were enough clean pages for our next case. Then I found a spot on my bookshelf for *The Detective's Bible*.

Before putting the book away, I looked through the *Rules of Sensible Sleuthing* one last time. The tenth and final rule was just three words long:

'Trust no one.'

This was not a lesson we were likely to forget.